U.S Department of Defense
Standards of Conduct Office

Encyclopedia

of Ethical Failure[1]

Revised September 2015

Contents

Introduction

The Standards of Conduct Office of the Department of Defense General Counsel's Office has assembled the following selection of cases of ethical failure for use as a training tool. Our goal is to provide DoD personnel with real examples of Federal employees who have intentionally or unwittingly violated the standards of conduct. Some cases are humorous, some sad, and all are real. Some will anger you as a Federal employee and some will anger you as an American taxpayer.

Please pay particular attention to the multiple jail and probation sentences, fines, employment terminations and other sanctions that were taken as a result of these ethical failures. Violations of many ethical standards involve *criminal* statutes. Protect yourself and your employees by learning what you need to know and accessing your Agency ethics counselor if you become unsure of the proper course of conduct. Be sure to access them *before* you take action regarding the issue in question. Many of the cases displayed in this collection could have been avoided completely if the offender had taken this simple precaution.

The cases have been arranged according to offense for ease of access. Feel free to reproduce and use them as you like in your ethics training program. For example - you may be conducting a training session regarding political activities. Feel free to copy and paste a case or two into your slideshow or handout – or use them as examples or discussion problems. If you have a case you would like to make available for inclusion in a future update of this collection, please email it to OSD.SOCO@MAIL.MIL or you may fax it to (703) 695-4970.

Disclaimer

The *Encyclopedia of Ethical Failure* is intended to sensitize Federal employees to the reach and impact of Federal ethics statutes and regulations. It is best used to supplement personal verification of those statutes and regulations. It should not be interpreted as a binding or authoritative presentation of the law.

Note of Special Thanks

We thank the DoD OIG for their case contributions to the Encyclopedia.

Abuse of Position

Subordinates Are Not Babysitters

A supervising attorney received a Letter of Caution for improperly requesting a subordinate paralegal perform a personal service. The supervisor, an ethics attorney no less, requested the subordinate paralegal pickup her child from daycare on her way home from work. The paralegal told investigators that, notwithstanding an emergency, she felt uncomfortable doing so given the appearance it might generate in the workplace. This was one of only a few requests spanning over a seven year period, but once is enough given the requirements levied by 5 C.F.R. § 2635.705 that govern use of official time and 5 C.F.R. § 2635.702 prohibiting the use of private office for public gain.

(Source: Department of Defense, Office of the Inspector General; 2015)

If I Help You Land This Multimillion Dollar Contract, Will You Give Me a Job?

A former government human resource director was sentenced to two years of probation for violating conflicts of interest laws, 18 U.S.C. § 208, and lying on his financial disclosure report. A whistleblower spilled the beans on a polling and market research firm's price inflation for government contracts and simultaneously its offer of a six-figure salary to the government official who was working to expand the firm's multimillion dollar contract with his agency. The former official was criminally sentenced to two-years of probation for failing to notify ethics officials about his employment arrangement with the firm on his financial disclosure report. In a related civil case, the former employee was barred from future government contracting work and forced to pay a $40,000 fine. Last but not least, the firm pulled his employment offer after the news broke.

General Discovers that Military Aides Are Not Supposed to Feed Cats

Military officials discovered that a General was misusing Government personnel, improperly accepting gifts of services from subordinates, and misusing his position. What did he do? The General used his enlisted aides to help host unofficial functions at his headquarters, provide driving lessons to a family member, and to feed a friend's cat. Although the aides were initially paid with $30-$40 Starbucks gift cards for their services, the General, taking full responsibility for his actions even though he retired, rectified the misuse and underpayment for services by retroactively paying the aides almost $2,000.

Misadventures in Hiring Family

Two retired colonels working for a National Guard educational program were found to have not been impartial in their duties when engaging in family hires. Colonel 1 nicely asked Colonel 2 to authorize the hiring of Colonel 1's son as a contractor which Colonel 2 did. Not to be outdone, Colonel 2 oversaw the hiring of his nephew and brother-in-law as contractors. Colonel 2 even attempted to get his own son hired as a contractor, but Colonel 2's supervisor correctly thought it would be inappropriate. Each colonel was issued a letter of caution to avoid an appearance of a conflict and they were required to take an annual ethics training course.

Chief Authority

A military service Chief Master Sergeant abused her authority and improperly used a government vehicle when she employed a government vehicle and three non-commissioned officers under her supervision to move personal property in a government rental vehicle. The soldiers helped her for 3 hours. The Chief Master Sergeant was given a verbal warning and advised of the improper use of government vehicles and the abuse of authority.

Abuse of Position and Bribery

A military service Captain used his official position as a reservist to obtain contracts for private sector companies with which he had an affiliation. In addition, the Captain accepted a "finder's fee" (i.e., kickbacks) from one company for his efforts in helping the company obtain government contract work. For his significant ethical failure, the Captain was "allowed" to retire at the grade of Commander, though he had been selected to be an Admiral. In addition, the Captain was debarred for one year, while two of the affiliated companies entered into administrative agreements (for 3 years) with the military service.

Coercion by Supervisor

The director of a naval health clinic received a $3,000 loan from a subordinate after requesting that the subordinate loan him $6,000. The $3,000 apparently wasn't enough, however, and the director later asked for $10,000. This time the subordinate declined. After the director only repaid a fraction of the $3,000, the subordinate approached the chain of command. In addition to being directed by his commanding officer to repay the rest of the loan, the director was provided with a written letter of counseling regarding his unprofessional and unethical conduct.

DoD GS-12 Removed for Misuse of Authority

A GS-12 Recreation Program Manager who supervised approximately 75 civilian and military subordinates was removed from his position for several ethical violations, including the failure to avoid the appearance of impropriety. The employee moved into visitors' quarters on a military installation where he stayed for six months without paying full price for his room by pressuring his subordinate to acquiesce to his payment arrangements. He also authorized an employee to make a $400 agency expenditure to purchase workout clothing for one MWR fitness instructor. The employee had no reason to believe he had the authority to authorize this expenditure and should have made inquiry before giving authorization. The administrative law judge stated that this act "at the very least gives the appearance of impropriety and should have raised a red flag."

Business Costs Employee

A former administrator for the Department of Health and Human Services took several trips on the government's dime that didn't look good. The advisor informed the HHS Secretary that he intended to seek employment in the private sector. The Secretary asked him to stay with the Department until Congress passed the new Medicare prescription drug benefits plan. The advisor agreed, but he continued to pursue his job search while serving as a government employee. While there is nothing wrong with government employees looking for a new job, the hang-up for this employee came when he decided to take several trips ostensibly related to his work for the HHS. While he was on these trips, he allegedly conducted "perfunctory meetings" for the HHS, and then he went off to do what he had really come to do—to have interviews with potential employers. Regardless of whether or not these trips were set up for the purpose of conducting bono fide government business, the advisor's meetings with potential employers during those trips gave the appearance that he was using his position for personal gain The employee has agreed to reimburse the government's costs for the trips, which totaled approximately $10,000 in value.

Federal Agent Demoted for I.D.ing Herself as a Federal Agent to a Police Officer

A Supervisory Special Agent for the Department of the Treasury (GS-14) was a passenger in a car that was pulled over by a local police officer. When the officer approached the vehicle, the employee presented the officer with her credentials identifying herself as a Federal Agent. The police officer had not asked to see the employee's identification at all. Because law enforcement officials may be tempted to treat other law enforcement officials more favorably, the Department determined the employee presented her government credentials to the police officer in hopes of receiving more favorable treatment. The federal employee did not explicitly ask the police officer for any favors, but the circumstances led her agency to the conclusion that she had attempted to use her official position for personal gain, which is prohibited by federal ethics rules. As a result, the employee's agency determined that she was untrustworthy as a supervisor and she was demoted.

Abuse of His Positions

A former ATF chief, Carl Truscott, was investigated by the Department of Treasury Inspector General and found to have committed numerous ethics violations. Among them, Truscott was found to have misused his position and to have wasted government resources by giving his nephew unlimited access to ATF employees and resources for a school project. The ATF's Office of Public Affairs staff was told by Truscott to comply with all of his nephew's requests. The OPA staff ended up "spoon feeding" Truscott's nephew. OPA staff spent numerous hours conducting research on publicly available information, mailing the nephew hard copies, providing the nephew with stock film footage, and conducting tours and interviews for the nephew. Truscott also asked employees at the Philadelphia field office to escort his nephew on tours, and to perform demonstrations of canine drug detection for him. When Truscott's nephew requested to visit the ATF headquarters, Truscott allowed him to use ATF equipment, including the ATF's film studio, cameras, and teleprompters to film interviews. Additionally,

Truscott gave his nephew three personal interviews, including once at the construction site of the new ATF building where Truscott, his assistant, and an OPA staff member had to travel to give the interview. Truscott also used his speechwriter to draft talking points for him to use in the interviews. And, as if that were not enough, after the nephew completed the video and received an "A" grade for it, Truscott continued to allow him to make requests to the ATF for suggestions on improving the video. One employee reported spending four or five days complying with the nephew's requests.

The IG was unable to tally the total number of employees and hours that were devoted to Truscott's nephew, but estimated that at least 20 ATF employees were involved. The IG determined that Truscott violated government regulations prohibiting federal employees from using their office for private gain, wasting government resources, and influencing subordinates to waste government resources. (Office of the Inspector General, Report of Investigation Concerning Alleged Mismanagement and Misconduct by Carl J. Truscott, Former Director of the Bureau of Alcohol, Tobacco, Firearms and Explosives.

SES Official's Involvement with Subordinate Leads to Retirement

The Inspector General found that an SES official engaged in an intimate relationship with a subordinate, provided her preferential treatment when selecting her for a new position, and misused Government resources and official time. The official retired before the IG completed his report. The IG report indicated that the official's relationship with a subordinate adversely affected the workplace, violated the requirements for members of the Senior Executive Service, and constituted conduct that was prejudicial to the Government. Witnesses noted that the official failed to hold his paramour accountable for her professional responsibilities, and when confronted by other employees, became verbally abusing, vengeful, and angry. The official also served as the selecting official, who selected his subordinate for promotion, while engaged in an intimate relationship with her, thereby violating the Merit system principles and engaging in a prohibited personal practice.

Affair with Assistant Leads to Employee Removal

A Deputy Assistant to the Secretary of Defense was terminated when investigators discovered that he had engaged in a romantic relationship with a DoD contractor who had served as his executive assistant. The executive assistant claimed that the end of their affair and the official's subsequent persistence had led her to leave her position. When questioned by investigators regarding the affair, the Deputy Assistant initially lied as to the nature of the relationship.

Although charges of sexual harassment could not be substantiated, the Inspector General found the Deputy Assistant's behavior to be incompatible with the standards of conduct established for DoD employees and members of the Senior Executive Service. The Office of the Secretary of Defense promptly initiated actions to terminate the Deputy Assistant.

DEA Agent - Misuse of Position

A DEA agent whose responsibilities included fleet management and authorization of repairs of Government vehicles had attempted to obtain free repair services for his personal vehicles from two vendors. The agent also insinuated to the vendors that the cost of repairing his personal vehicles could be recouped as part of the charges for repairs to Government vehicles. After these allegations were substantiated, the agent was dismissed from DEA.

Improper Use of Position

The Department of Justice Office of Professional Responsibility (OPR) investigated allegations that a Department of Justice (DOJ) attorney prepared another person's application for a visa with a cover memorandum on DOJ stationery. The DOJ attorney also included one of his DOJ business cards in the submission. The foreign individual was seeking a visa in order to enter the country to perform certain functions for a non-profit organization. The DOJ attorney told OPR that he did not intend to gain preferential treatment for the visa applicant by identifying himself as a DOJ attorney, but believed his actions were consistent with what DOJ employees are permitted to do on behalf of non-profit organizations.

OPR concluded that the actions of the DOJ attorney were improper, but not intentionally so. Section 2635.703 of the Standards of Ethical Conduct for Employees of the Executive Branch prohibits employees from using their position or title for purposes of endorsement.

"You obviously don't know who I am."

The son of a bureau director was denied a rental car because he was too young. Outraged, his father wrote a scathing letter (on Agency letterhead) to the president of the rental car company, and sent it off in a U.S. postage-paid envelope. The president of the company was not amused and returned his scathing response to the head of the Agency. As a result of his action, the Bureau Director was treated to a four-hour ethics session and a fine for personal use of official postage.

"But, Judge, I didn't get anything!"

An offshore safety inspector found much of the Government's equipment to be in need of repairs to meet safety standards. He then referred the business to his brother-in-law's repair shop. The rig operators smelled a rat and called the FBI. They discovered that, in return for each referral, the brother-in-law was treating the inspector to an evening with a lady of dubious morals.

The case was brought to trial. In his defense, the inspector claimed that he had not received a "thing of value" in return for the referral. The judge didn't buy it - and neither did his wife.

Use of Contractor Time

Allegations were made against a Department of Defense (DoD) official regarding his use of contractor employees. The official directed two US Government contractors to entertain an acquaintance he met at a conference in Europe on his behalf. They were directed to take the person out to lunch as well as out on the town the following evening. The contractors rightly believed that the request was improper and as a result told the DoD official that they "had other plans." The DoD official told them to "cancel them." The contractors eventually took the acquaintance out that evening for several hours.

After an investigation, it was determined that the DoD official had acted in violation of 5 CFR 2635.704 by utilizing contractors' time improperly. His supervisor counseled him and the proper reimbursements were made.

Veterans Affairs Supervisors Push for Friends to be Hired

A review found in two instances that Department of Veterans Affairs medical center supervisors recommended the hiring of close personal friends without divulging the relationship to human resources staff members. The review team recommended that disciplinary action be taken.

Interior Official Altered Reports and Leaked Confidential Information

The Interior Department's Inspector General found that a senior official had repeatedly altered scientific field reports to lessen the protections for imperiled species and ease the impact on landowners. The investigation also revealed the official, who works in Fish and Wildlife Services, misused her position by disclosing confidential information to private groups seeking to affect policy decisions. The Inspector General referred the case to the Department Head for "potential administrative action."

(The Seattle Times, March 30, 2007)

Bribery (18 U.S.C. § 201-Type Violations)

Former Sperry Executive Pleads Guilty on Navy Bribe

A former Sperry executive pled guilty in Federal District Court on charges that he bribed a Navy official for help in competing for an electronics contract. The Navy official, who pled guilty as well, received over $400,000 for his efforts in proposing and promoting the company, which was deposited into a Bahama bank account. The dramatic irony for those implicated is that, despite the Navy official's efforts, Sperry was eliminated from the contract competition.

These guilty pleas were just a few of the more than 20 other convictions resulting from a DOJ investigation into military procurement fraud. Sentences have included a 32-month jail term for a separate bribery scheme initiated by another Sperry executive and a 27-month term for the "banker" in that case. Moral of the story: it doesn't pay to bribe.

(Source: AP; published 21 Oct 1989)

Retirement Does Not Guarantee "Prosecution Free"

A former regional Department of Housing and Urban Development office director received $38,000 in paybacks from the recipient of a government loan totaling $1.5 million. The director was initially placed on administrative leave before retiring from the agency. That did not prevent him from escaping the long-arm of the law, however, as he is currently serving an 18-month prison sentence for conspiracy to provide and accept an illegal gratuity.

(Source: The Washington Post; published 4 Feb 2015)

My Oath of Office for Your Cold Hard Cash

A U.S. Foreign Service officer, who worked in the U.S. Consulate in Ho Chi Minh City, Vietnam, was responsible for issuing visas after reviewing applications and conducting interviews. He conspired with U.S. and Vietnamese citizens to recruit customers who would pay $15,000 to $70,000 in exchange for non-immigrant visas from Vietnam to the U.S. He accepted over $3 million in bribes and allowed nearly 500 foreign nationals to enter the U.S. He pleaded guilty to bribery and agreed to pay at least $6 million in a money judgment and faces up to 24 years in prison.

The Godfather

A former Department of Defense employee used to refer to himself as "The Godfather" because of his ability to influence the awarding of construction contracts. However, like all great crime bosses, this employee was arrested for extorting a $10,000 bribe. The Godfather accepted a $10,000 installment of a $40,000 bribe from an undercover agent in an attempt to secure a flooring contract. The Godfather was taken into custody.

Lucrative Contracting

A former Army officer had found a lucrative gig: accepting cash payments for facilitating contracting between Iraqis and the U.S. government during a deployment to Baghdad. This particular officer accepted $37,500 in cash payment for these "facilitations." The officer was sentenced to prison, three years of supervised release, and was required to pay $37,500 restitution to the U.S. Government.

Bribe for a Bulldozer

A retired military employee plead guilty to taking bribes in exchange for turning a blind eye while others stole heavy equipment from the base for resale. The man admitted to allowing items such as cranes, bulldozers, and front-end loaders to be taken from the base. As part of his plea agreement, the employee agreed to forfeit the bribe proceeds, as well as to pay full restitution to the Department of Defense.

Fraud, Conspiracy, and Bribery ... Oh My!

Criminal charges put a computer contractor out of business and landed government employees in jail. Two civilian employees at a Military Depot, along with the contractor's government sales manager, were convicted on various conspiracy and bribery charges for defrauding the U.S. Government under multiple contracts in return for cash and merchandise. The employees were part of a scheme in which they used government funds to purchase laptops and recycled computer components from the contractor's sales manager at inflated prices, and split the overcharged amounts among themselves. One employee received prison time, three years probation, and was ordered to pay $30,000 in restitution. The other employee was sentenced to 22 months in jail, three years of probation, and ordered to pay $18,000. The sales manager received a similar sentence. The computer contractor was indicted on nine felony counts and subjected to asset forfeiture of approximately $7.8 million. The charges were later withdrawn after the company filed for bankruptcy. The investigation also resulted in five other individuals charged with prison time and ordered to pay a combined $127,000 in restitution.

One Thing Leads to Another

A misuse of government resources investigation hit unexpected pay dirt when it uncovered a contractor procurement and bribery scheme. Investigators responding to a hotline tip substantiated a misuse of funds claim when they found a civilian utilities manager at a Military command rented a 350-ton crane to move electrical generators seven days before it was needed; costing the government $35,000. The investigation also uncovered a complicated contract bid rigging, bribery and kickback operation involving the utilities manager and a Service contractor. The manager manipulated and sole-sourced work to the contractor; reportedly to drive business to the contractor in order to transition to a job with them after his government job. The manager used government funds to purchase expensive tools, plasma TVs, and laptop computers that turned up missing. He also allowed the contractor to use government personnel, tools, and equipment to do the contractor's work. He submitted false invoices on behalf of the contractor, resulting in a $1.3 million loss to the government. As a result of a plea deal for cooperation in additional procurement investigations, the manager was sentenced to 15 months in prison and debarred from government contracting for four years. This investigation touched off five separate criminal investigations against other contractors in that Military Service regarding allegations of bid rigging.

Bribery and Fraud Lands Program Manager in Jail

A Program Manager (PM) that was responsible for administering computer contracts received kickbacks and ran his own business defrauding the Government. The PM negotiated a deal with a contractor that raised the price of computer storage equipment by $500 a unit. The increase was for "additional services" that were supposedly needed to resolve a defect in the equipment. An investigation determined that these services were unnecessary, and that the $500 was paid to a shell company owned by the PM's wife.

The $500 per unit was just the start. He also used a business that he controlled to purchase generic equipment and resell it to the Government as a name brand product far above market rate. These endeavors proved to be quite lucrative, and the PM profited about $3.2 million on the schemes. The profit was short-lived, however, as the PM was indicted for bribery and fraud. He was sentenced to five years in prison, required to repay the $3.2 million and charged a $2,400 fine.

Contracting Official in Afghanistan Pleads Guilty to Bribery

A Government employee at Bagram Airfield, pled guilty to accepting bribes in exchange for awarding Government contracts. The employee was responsible for evaluating trucking contractors and assigning each contractor days of work each month based on their performance. The employee was approached by a contractor and ultimately accepted a wireless telephone and $20,000 a month in exchange for assigning an extra day of work each month to that contractor. He also made a similar deal with another contractor for $15,000 a month. In all, the employee received about $87,000. He was sentenced to forty months in prison and three years of supervised release.

Major Wrongdoing

A retired Army Major, Christopher H. Murray, pled guilty to charges of bribery and making a false statement arising from his activities at Camp Arifjan, Kuwait.

In 2005 and 2006, while serving as a contracting specialist at Camp Arijan, Murray received approximately $225,000 in bribes from DOD contractors. In return, he recommended

14

the award of contracts for various goods and services. Murray also admitted that he received an additional $20,000 in bribes from a DOD contractor in exchange for the award of a construction contract. Murray's misconduct continued as he made false statements to federal agents investigating his conduct. Murray's sentencing is pending, but the maximum penalty for each of four bribery counts is 15 years in prison and a $250,000 fine. The maximum penalty for making a false statement is five years in prison and a $250,000 fine.

In another bribery case at Camp Arifjan, another Army Major, James Momon, Jr., accepted cash bribes from five DOD contracting firms that supplied bottled water and other goods and services to bases in Kuwait. Momon, a contracting officer at the camp, awarded contracts and Blanket Purchase Agreement calls to those contractors, receiving $5.8 million as payment for his actions. Momon pled guilty to bribery and conspiracy to commit bribery. His sentencing is pending, but, like Murray, Momon faces up to 15 years in prison and a $250,000 fine for each bribery count, as well as five years in prison for the conspiracy count. Momon has also agreed to pay $5.8 million in restitution.

Inhibiting Victory

A Major in the U.S. Army Reserve pled guilty to conspiracy and bribery charges related to DOD contracts at Camp Victory, Iraq. According to the charging document, Theresa Jeanne Baker received money and other items, including a Harley Davidson motorcycle, from a defense contractor, Raman Corporation, and a former employee of another defense contractor, Elie Samir Chidiac. In return, Baker conveyed sensitive information and fraudulently awarded contracts to the contractor. Baker also canceled contracts that were awarded to third party contractors and fraudulently re-awarded them to Chidiac. Baker's sentencing is pending, but the maximum penalty for each of Baker's two bribery counts is 15 years in prison and the greater of a $250,000 fine and three times the monetary equivalent of the thing of value received. Baker was also charged with two counts of conspiracy. Each count comes with a maximum penalty of five years in prison and a $250,000 fine.

Courting Trouble

A former official of the U.S. Tax Court, Fred Fernando Timbol Jr., was sentenced to 18 months in prison and three years of supervised release in connection with a bribery conspiracy.

Timbol was a facilities services officer in the Facilities Management Section of the U.S. Tax Court. Timbol was responsible for assisting in the award of contracts to contractors who provided maintenance, construction, and other related service to the Court. Timbol admitted to soliciting and accepting over $12,000 from a government contractor in exchange for rigging the award of at least six inflated contracts. As part of a plea agreement and by order of the court, Timbol also agreed to pay restitution of $24,143.

Moore Misconduct

First Lieutenant Robert Moore (Ret.) agreed to pay $120,000 in restitution for accepting money from contractors in exchange for the award of DOD contracts.

In addition to pleading guilty to bribery for the award of contracts at Bagram Airfield, Afghanistan, Moore pled guilty to conspiracy, admitting to falsifying the number of bunkers and barriers delivered at Bagram, which resulted in DOD paying for bunkers and barriers that were never received. Moore also admitted falsifying damage reports for leased vehicles, causing DOD to pay for repairs not performed.

Two other officials, Christopher P. West, an Army Major, and Patrick W. Boyd, an Air Force Master Sergeant, likewise pled guilty to bribery and conspiracy for related conduct. The two agreed to pay $500,000 and $130,000, respectively, in restitution to DOD.

Department Employee Works to the Public Detriment

A civilian Engineering Technician assigned to the Public Works Department at Naval Air Station, Corpus Christi, TX recommended Contract Construction and Fence Company for a $153,000 contract. But behind the scenes, the company had first agreed to pay the Government employee $5,000 in exchange for the recommendation, per the employee's request. The technician admitted to accepting the bribe in return for his official action that resulted in the contract award. The Navy debarred the civilian employee for three years, and he left Federal service.

VA Employee Earns a 46-Month Stay in the Slammer for Corruption

A Department of Veterans Affairs employee was caught demanding and receiving kickbacks from a contractor doing business with her agency. The VA employee and the contractor agreed that the employee would recommend the contractor's services to her agency, and in return the contractor would give the employee kickbacks from the inflated prices it charged the government. In all, the employee received $115,000 in kickbacks, although the scheme ended up costing the government much more—between $400,000 and $1 million. On a side note, the VA employee was also indicted for conducting post-government employment negotiations with a company she was doing business with in her government capacity.

Accepting Gifts from Vendor Results in $1,000 Fine

A U.S. Postal Service (USPS) employee who accepted free tee time golf games from a vendor had to explain his actions in Federal court after a tipster informed investigators. Authorities learned that the employee, who was the manager of Delivery Vehicle Operations, had played golf with a vendor who was involved in a $100 million procurement with USPS. On that occasion, the employee had accepted payment for his golf fees and his dinner. Investigators discovered that over the course of the previous year, the employee had also accepted approximately $2,000 in non-cash items (including meals and golf fees) from the vendor.

The employee pled guilty to bribery, and was sentenced to one year unsupervised probation and a $1,000 fine. For this employee, golf turned into a very expensive sport.

Exchanging Contract for Computer Earns Prison Time

The Facts: The director of Respiratory Care at a Veterans Affairs (VA) hospital in Shreveport, Louisiana, agreed to push through a VA contract for a vendor, if the vendor supplied her with a laptop computer. The VA Police and Security Service, as they are wont to do, investigated and discovered this *quid pro quo*. The director was caught and pleaded guilty to soliciting and receiving illegal gifts. She was sentenced to 5 months in prison, to be followed by 7 months of home confinement, and ordered to pay restitution of $904. (Source: *Federal Ethics Report*, Feb. 2001.)

The Law: 18 U.S.C. § 201(c)(1)(B) (2003) forbids any public official from accepting anything of value in exchange for an official act to be performed, or because of any official act already performed. Violations of this law can merit fines, imprisonment for up to 2 years, or both.

Asking for a Bribe — Have You Lost Your Mind?

The Facts: An employee at the Defense MegaCenter at Kelly Air Force Base, Texas, was working as a member of a source evaluation committee reviewing contract proposals for a $5 million contract when he struck on this ingenious idea: Ask one of the potential contractors for a bribe in exchange for his approval of the contractor's proposal! The contractor apparently didn't think that this was such a good idea, however. It contacted the Defense Criminal Investigative Service, which investigated the case along with the Air Force. The investigation included using an undercover agent, parading as the contractor's representative, paying the employee the bribe. Having been caught with his hand in the cookie jar, the employee pleaded guilty to accepting a bribe and was sentenced to one year of probation and ordered to participate in a mental health program—perhaps an appropriate remedy for what proved to be a lame-brained scheme. (Source: *Federal Ethics Report*, Feb. 2001.)

The Law: 18 U.S.C. § 201(b)(2)(A) (2003) bars public officials and any persons selected to be public officials from seeking anything of value in return for "being influenced . . . in the performance of any official act." The penalty for violating this law can include fines, imprisonment for up to 15 years, or both, along with possible disqualification from holding "any office of honor, trust, or profit" with the United States Government.

Don't Be Too Gracious a Gift-Getter !

The Facts: An employee of the Maritime Administration (MARAD), a division of the Department of Transportation, oversaw contracts for ship repairs. He also saw a contractor providing him with nice gifts to reward his work—including a large-screen TV and a VCR. What could be wrong with that? Plenty, according to the U.S. Attorney, who delivered to this gracious gift-getter a four-month prison sentence, to be followed by one year of probation, and an order for restitution in the amount of $7,460. The other gifts the employee could have refused; these he was compelled to take. (Source: *Federal Ethics Report*, Feb. 2001.)

The Law: 18 U.S.C. § 201(c)(1)(B) (2003) forbids any public official from accepting anything of value in exchange for an official act, or given for an official act already taken. A violation of this law can result in fines, imprisonment for up to 2 years, or both.

Not So Much of a Bright Bulb !

The Facts: A former supervisor in the Bureau of Indian Affairs used a Government-issue credit card to purchase excessive quantities of overpriced light bulbs from a North Dakota company. In exchange for his act as a poor shopper, he accepted $21,000 in bribes. For his savvy purchasing, he was sentenced to one year and nine months in prison and ordered to pay $72,000 in restitution.

The Law: 18 U.S.C. § 201(b) (2003) forbids Federal employees from (among other things) seeking or receiving anything of value in return for being influenced in the performance of an official act or to commit or to assist the commission of any fraud against the United States. It mandates fines, imprisonment for up to 15 years, or both, along with disqualification from holding "any office of honor, trust, or profit under the United States."

FAA Employee Sentenced for Bribery

A former employee of the Federal Aviation Administration (FAA) was convicted of bribery. In carrying out his primary responsibility of reviewing and processing applications for FAA-issued pilot certificates, the employee accepted bribes of $2,000 and an all-expense paid trip to Korea in exchange for preferential treatment of applications for Korean pilots from the flight school, Wings Over America.

The employee was sentenced to pay a $2,000 fine and serve four months in prison, followed by three years probation for violating 18 U.S.C. 201(b)(2). Bribery occurs when a public official seeks or accepts anything of value in return for being influenced in the performance of an official act.

Social Security Administration Employee's Bribery Try Ends in Prison

A Social Security Administration employee and her husband were convicted for soliciting bribes from individuals seeking Social Security benefits for themselves or family members. The couple approached citizens who were having difficulty qualifying for Supplemental Social Security benefits. They would offer to arrange to have benefits reinstated or to complete paperwork for the individual. Afterwards, they demanded payment for their services.

At their 1997 trial in Louisiana, a judge ordered the employee to 46 months imprisonment followed by three years of probation. The employee's husband received 30 months imprisonment, also followed by three years of probation. They each paid back $23,809.33.

The offense of bribery occurs when a public official seeks or accepts anything of value in return for being influenced in the performance of an official act.

Navy Employee Sentenced for Gratuity Offense

A Navy electrical foreman was sentenced for accepting $9,300 in illegal gratuities from a Government contractor. The foreman was convicted of violating 18 U.S.C. 201 and was sentenced to 36 months of probation and a $10,000 fine. The electrical foreman assisted a Government contractor in obtaining a contract with the Naval Air Warfare Center (NAWC). The foreman had authority over certain Navy contracts relating to NAWC base maintenance.

Congressional Aide Sentenced for Corrupt Activities

A former staff assistant to a U.S. Congressman was convicted of two counts of accepting gratuities (18 U.S.C. 201) and one count of devising and carrying out a scheme to defraud the Government (18 U.S.C. 1341). The aide was sentenced to 18 months imprisonment on each count followed by two years of probation. The staff assistant accepted $3,700 for assisting individuals in obtaining permanent residency status by sending endorsements on the Congressman's letterhead to the Immigration and Naturalization Service (INS). The aide was also involved in a scheme to defraud aliens seeking permanent residency. The aide told the aliens that if they were members in the Seventh Day Adventist Church, they would be eligible for permanent resident status even though the INS Special Religious Immigrant Work Program covers only church workers and their immediate families who are employed by a religious organization. The aliens were informed that for a fee, the aide would assist them in applying with the INS. The aide received approximately $400,000 from 1,000 aliens.

HUD Official and Realtor Imprisoned for Bribery Scheme

A former official at the U.S. Department of Housing and Urban Development (HUD) was sentenced for his role in a bribery scheme involving HUD properties. The former official was paid bribes by a realtor who in exchange was sold HUD properties at lower than their appraised values. The bribes totaled over $80,000, including a BMW automobile. In return the HUD official sold the realtor 20 HUD properties at one-third of their appraised value. The realtor then resold the properties at their full market value. In addition to other charges, both the HUD official and the realtor plead guilty to one count of 18 U.S.C. 201 each.

The HUD official was sentenced to a 24-month prison term followed by 3 years probation and was ordered to pay $1.4 million in restitution. The realtor was sentenced to a 27-month prison term followed by 3 years probation and was also ordered to pay $1.4 million in restitution.

United States Customs Service Special Agent Takes Informant Payoff Funds

Beginning in June 1987, the agent worked with an informant who provided assistance to the Customs Service in criminal investigations. One of the agent's duties was to monitor and assess the work of the informant. During a period of several years, the informant received a number of payments from the Customs Service as compensation for his services as informant. On one or more occasions, the informant expressed gratitude for the agent's assistance by observing that both he and the agent had engaged in hard work for which the informant would receive substantial compensation, but for which the agent only would receive his salary. The informant offered to share with the agent a portion of his earnings from the Customs Service. In April 1992, the agent nominated the informant for a large payment, which represented a portion of the value of certain assets forfeited as a result of information provided by the informant. The agent then initiated a telephone conversation with the informant in which he asked the informant for money. During August 1992, the informant went to San Francisco to receive the payment. The agent personally gave the informant a United States Treasury check in the amount of $110,875. While riding in a Government-owned vehicle, the informant attempted to hand the agent an envelope with $4,000 in cash. The agent responded that the informant should drop the envelope in the car because he could not accept the cash directly. The informant left the money in the car and the agent recovered it.

The agent pled guilty pursuant to a plea agreement to a charge of a criminal violation of 18 U.S.C. 209, illegal supplementation of salary. Under the plea agreement, the agent agreed to the imposition of a fine of $4,000 by the Court, to not seek employment with any Federal, state, or local law enforcement Agency, and to pay a special assessment of $25. In exchange for these agreements, the United States agreed to move to dismiss the Indictment charging the agent with a violation of 18 U.S.C. 201(c)(1)(B) and not to prosecute him for any other criminal offense relating to his receipt of $4,000 from the informant.

Gratuity Accepted In Exchange for Immigration Services

A pastor submitted an application for permanent residence to the United States Department of Justice, Immigration and Naturalization Service (INS). The Southeastern Conference of Seventh-Day Adventists (Southeastern Conference) wanted the pastor to minister to two of its congregations in Miami. On August 17, 1990, a Congressman sent a letter to INS on behalf of the pastor. On May 31, 1991, a second letter from the Congressman, this time signed by the pastor as well, was sent to INS. Both letters were written on Congressional stationery. On August 21, 1991, the pastor's application for permanent residence was approved. On July 8, 1993, the Congressional staffer who organized the scheme received a $500 gratuity from the Southeastern Conference for her efforts on behalf of the pastor. The staffer used the same scheme to assist another pastor in obtaining permanent residence so that he could serve as minister for two of the Southeastern Conference's congregations. The Congressman wrote to INS on July 26, 1993, on behalf of the second pastor and the Southeastern Conference. The staffer assisted the second pastor in his dealings with INS. On August 3, 1993, INS approved the pastor's petition for residence and, on February 3, 1994, the staffer received a $500 gratuity from the Southeastern Conference for her efforts on behalf of the pastor. On April 26, 1994, another foreign national paid the staffer $2,700 for assisting her in applying for permanent residence. The staffer submitted a petition to INS on the person's behalf and signed the application as the preparer. Although the application contained a signature, which purported to be that of the staffer, she claimed that it was not her signature and that she did not see the application prior to its submission. The staffer knew that the foreign national was not eligible to become a permanent resident of the U.S. but fraudulently misrepresented to her that she was eligible in order to induce her to utilize the staffer's services.

The staffer was charged with two counts of accepting gratuities for official acts performed, in violation of 18 U.S.C. 201(c)(1)(B) and knowingly making a material false writing and presenting it to INS, in violation of 18 U.S.C. 1001. She was also charged with accepting compensation for services provided in relation to matters in which the United States has a direct and substantial interest, in violation of 18 U.S.C. 203(a)(1), and mail fraud, in violation of 18 U.S.C. 1341. The staffer pled guilty to the five-count indictment on September 30, 1996, and was sentenced to 18 months of incarceration on April 18, 1997.

Multiple Charges Brought Against Air Force Officer and Accomplice for Software Scheme

An Air Force officer was disgruntled after receiving notification that he would not be promoted and was soon to be discharged without a retirement annuity. He conspired with a base warehouse supervisor (while also seeking employment with him) to unlawfully transfer superseded software from the MacDill AFB warehouse he supervised to a private company for subsequent sale. He arranged with the supervisor to remove software called Oracle Tools and Database (Oracle). The Air Force officer obtained possession of over 96 boxes of Oracle software by making false statements in writing in an effort to gain authorization from his superiors to have the software destroyed in place. Destruction of superseded software was the responsibility of the Government according to its agreements with software contractors. The Air Force officer worked under the pretense that the Oracle software was being turned over to a company for destruction. Instead, the officer provided the Oracle software to a moving company that transported the boxes from MacDill to a commercial storage facility rented by the warehouse supervisor. Once in possession of the software, he searched for buyers of the software. Originally, the U.S. Central Command had paid the Government bulk rate of $79,000 for the Oracle software in 1991. On the gray market, this software was valued between $35,000 and $100,000.

The officer was convicted of a violation of 18 U.S.C. 208 (working on a project that affected a company in which he had a financial interest), while his co-defendant, the warehouse supervisor, was convicted of violations of 18 U.S.C. 201(b)(1), 18 U.S.C. 641 (theft of Government property) and 18 U.S.C. 371 (conspiracy). The officer was sentenced to one year probation and 150 hours community service. The warehouse supervisor was imprisoned for 27 months with supervised release for three years.

State Department Regional Security Officer (RSO) at the American Embassy in Santo Domingo, Dominican Republic Drives Automobile Scheme

The RSO's primary duties included overseeing a small force of U.S. Marines and a larger force of security guards. While the RSO had no authority to enter into procurement transactions on the Government's behalf, he did, in two separate transactions, engineer the purchase of eight vehicles for the security company and some private citizens. The security company's contract with the Government required that it use three vehicles for patrols. These vehicles were purchased in the United States and were free from substantial import duties when delivered to the Dominican Republic by virtue of applications by the United States Embassy for "exonerations" from the duties. Exonerations are given for property to be used by foreign missions. With respect to the purchase of the first four vehicles, the RSO was given $50,000 by the security company. The RSO carried at least $39,000 in cash to Miami, which he illegally failed to disclose to customs officials, and purchased 4 vehicles for $39,000. The RSO kept the remaining $11,000. Later, when the RSO purchased four vehicles for individuals, he was given $55,000 in cash. He returned to Miami with at least $35,000 in cash, which again he failed to report to Customs, and paid $35,000 for four vehicles which were sent to Santo Domingo and "exonerated" from import duty after the RSO encouraged the exoneration process and initiated some of the paperwork through an embassy employee. The RSO retained the unspent $20,000 difference between the purchase amount and the amount he had been given to purchase the cars. The security company also was required to provide weapons for its security force. The RSO arranged to purchase the weapons for the security company by first attempting to have certain firearm companies or retailers ship the weapons to the Dominican Republic, notwithstanding the fact that the RSO did not have a license to export the weapons. These companies refused to sell the weapons to the RSO. Subsequently, he purchased the weapons from a Baltimore gun shop after using Embassy letterhead and representing that he was authorized to purchase weapons for the State Department. The gun shop refused to ship the weapons to the RSO. The RSO then went to Baltimore and personally purchased the weapons and sent them in a lead-lined diplomatic box to the Dominican Republic. The RSO gave most of the weapons to the security company, but sold some extras that he purchased to citizens of the Dominican Republic at considerable profit. He also kept for himself the difference of $2000 between the amount that the security company had given him to purchase the guns and the amount that the gun purchase had cost him.

The RSO was charged with making false statements to a firearms dealer, receiving something of value for performance of an official act in violation of 18 U.S.C. 201, participating as a Government employee in a transaction in which he had a financial interest in violation of 18 U.S.C. 208, stealing ammunition with a value in excess of $100 from the United States, exporting firearms without a license, transporting monetary instruments into the United States for the purpose of carrying on a violation of the Arms Control Export Act, and failing to make a true report to the Customs Service when carrying $10,000 or more into the United States. The jury convicted the RSO on the 201 count and the count of the indictment pertaining to exporting firearms without a license.

Postal Employee Demanded Payoffs to Deliver Benefit Checks

Having been tipped off that a letter carrier was demanding money from people on his route in exchange for delivery of general assistance checks, the Postal Service established surveillance and taped a conversation in which the letter carrier suggested that the customer make a "one-time" payment of $15 to ensure delivery of her checks. The letter carrier accepted the payment, which had been marked in advance of its transfer. The letter carrier was indicted under 18 U.S.C. 201(c)(1)(B) for accepting money in exchange for performing an official duty. After plea negotiations, he pled guilty to a violation of 18 U.S.C. 209, for accepting compensation for official duties from a source other than the Government. He was sentenced to three years' probation, with 60 days at a community treatment center.

Employee Convicted for Steering Contracts to Supplier

A Government technician and a co-worker went to a manufacturer and offered to ensure that the manufacturer received Agency contracts in return for a hefty "finder's fee." The manufacturer, unfortunately for these enterprising employees, went to the FBI, which set up a sting operation and arrested the technician. At trial, the technician, ever so clever, argued that he could not be found guilty of bribery because he was not a contracting officer, and therefore did not have the authority to award contracts to the manufacturer. The court rejected this argument after listening to testimony on the role of technicians as far as providing expert information that contracting officers rely upon, and upheld the conviction of the technician.

The offense of bribery occurs when a public official seeks or accepts anything of value in return for being influenced in the performance of an official act. Such acts include giving advice, making recommendations, and conducting investigations as well as making decisions.

Please Call Me "Doctor" Inmate

One enterprising Federal employee cut a deal with a local university - they gave him an honorary Ph.D. in public administration in return for his signing a mega-buck grant for the university. (Obviously, he had great expertise in Public Administration.)

The offense of bribery occurs when a public official seeks or accepts anything of value (such as an honorary degree) in return for being influenced in the performance of an official act.

Agriculture Employee Sought for Approving Fraudulent Loans

A former employee of the Department of Agriculture is wanted for recruiting his friends to fraudulently apply for farm loans and then giving him money in exchange for approving the loans. The former employee helped his non-farmer co-conspirators to fill out the required forms with the information required for approval. Under this scheme, the former employee approved loans totaling $1.8 million. He collected $340,000 for himself.

The former employee has been charged with 98 counts including 56 for bribery.

Seven Agriculture Inspectors Sentenced for Bribery Scheme

Seven U.S. Department of Agriculture fruit and vegetable inspectors were convicted of operating a scheme in which they received cash payments from fruit and vegetable wholesalers in return for the inspectors assigning lower grades to their produce. The lower grade meant that the wholesaler could pay the grower a lower price for the produce and then re-sell it at the higher grade.

All pled guilty to one count of bribery each. Bribery occurs when a public official seeks or accepts anything of value (such as cash) in return for being influenced in the performance of an official act (such as assigning produce grades).

INS Inspector Accepts Bribes

A former Immigration and Naturalization Service inspector was sentenced for accepting bribes in return for allowing smugglers to import cocaine into the United States across the border with Mexico. He accepted $75,000 in bribes in return for allowing over 1,000 pounds of cocaine to enter the country.

The former INS inspector was convicted of bribery and was sentenced to 30 months imprisonment followed by three years of probation.

Former Federal Highway Administration Official and Wife Engage in Corrupt Scheme

A former FHWA employee and his wife were sentenced for engaging in a bribery and kickback scheme involving traffic engineering contracts. The former employee improperly told a contractor that they would probably win a contract. In return, the contractor granted a sub-contract to the FHWA employee's wife's "consulting firm." The employee's wife had no highway engineering education or experience. She received over $100,000 in Government contracts.

In addition to other charges, the former employee pled guilty to one count of bribery.

VA Employee Convicted of Accepting Illegal Gratuities

A former employee of the U.S. Department of Veterans Affairs was sentenced for soliciting and accepting gratuities from a VA vendor. He received three computers, airline tickets, and hotel accommodations from several VA vendors. He was also charged with demanding a fourth computer and round trip tickets to Las Vegas from another vendor. The former employee pled guilty to one count of violation of 18 U.S.C. 201.

IRS Official Convicted for Steering Contracts

A former IRS official was sentenced in US District Court for accepting bribes in return for directing IRS computing contracts to certain companies and for failing to report the bribes on his income tax returns.

He pled guilty to one count of bribery and to one count of filing a false tax return, and received a 37 month prison term and three years' probation as a result. Bribery occurs when a public official seeks or accepts anything of value in return for being influenced in the performance of an official act.

Special Operations Command Bribery Scandal Nabs Two Retired Officers

Two retired military officers at SOCOM found themselves in federal court after the revelation of a scheme to funnel defense contracts to companies willing to provide lucrative kickbacks. The first official was a retired Army lieutenant colonel, and was employed by SOCOM as a contractor charged with evaluating weapons designed for the special operations forces. The second official was a retired Army colonel, who was chief of special programs at SOCOM. Prosecutors allege that the retired colonel formed a private consulting company in order to represent companies seeking to get part of SOCOM's $1.8 billion procurement budget. The consulting company then made illegal payments to the retired lieutenant colonel in exchange for his favorable reviews of their clients' weapons.

The retired lieutenant colonel pled guilty to federal bribery charges. Although he faced 15 years in prison, his exemplary service and cooperation with investigators earned him a reduced sentence of three years of supervised probation, six months of home detention, and $4500 in fines. The retired colonel has maintained his innocence, and faces up to 15 years in prison and $250,000 in fines.

Iraq Contractor Caught Taking $1 Million in Bribes

A former contracting officer for the Iraqi coalition government pled guilty to accepting over $1 million in bribes in return for steering contracts to a contractor with companies in Iraq and Romania. The officer was a convicted felon when he was hired by a U.S. company, which subsequently won a contract with the U.S. to provide controllers to Iraqi regions. The officer was put in charge of over $82 million in funding for an area south of Baghdad. He quickly began accepting bribes in the form of cash, cars, jewelry, and sexual favors from women provided by a contractor, in exchange for steering lucrative contracts in the contractor's direction. Investigators recovered incriminating email traffic, including one email from the official to the contractor exclaiming, "I love to give you money!" Later investigations showed that much of the contracted work was never completed. Also implicated in the scandal was a retired Army lieutenant colonel, who also worked as a contracting officer in the region. He was accused of funneling contracts to the same contractor in exchange for lucrative kickbacks, including a new car; he also was accused of simply stealing large amounts of money from reconstruction funds which he then smuggled into the U.S.

The official pled guilty to bribery, conspiracy, and money-laundering, as well as charges connected with his illegal possession of at least 50 firearms, including machine guns and grenade launchers. He awaits sentencing, and faces up to 30 years for the conspiracy charge alone. The contractor pled guilty to conspiracy, bribery, and money-laundering. He faces up to 40 years in prison, five years of supervised release and a fine of $750,000. He also must repay the government $3.6 million and forfeit $3.6 million in assets. The lieutenant colonels case is still pending. *(Source: Washington Post, February 2, 2006; April 16, 2006)*

Cargo Contractor Faces 5 Years for Bribery

A Navy contractor at the Space and Naval Warfare Systems Center Charleston Detachment pled guilty to accepting bribes from a freight forwarding company. In exchange for awarding freight transportation contracts to the company, the contractor received items valued at more than $10,000, including extravagant dinners, concert and NASCAR tickets, weekends at a bed-and-breakfast, jewelry, and "spa days" at a department store. Investigators discovered that coincidentally, the freight company's business was virtually nonexistent before the contractor began awarding them contracts that eventually totaled over $700,000.

The contractor faces up to five years in prison and a $250,000 fine. She is the seventh defendant connected to an investigation of payoffs between freight forwarding companies and government contractors. *(Source: UPI, March 20, 2006)*

Gift-Giving Contractor Faces 5 Years for Bribery

The owner of a cargo company in Virginia Beach faces five years in prison after giving thousands of dollars in gifts to federal contract officers at the Norfolk Naval Shipyard in exchange for lucrative military shipping contracts. One federal contract officer, who had worked for the government for 25 years, received free lunches and dinners, an open tab at a delicatessen, airline tickets, concert and NASCAR tickets, cigars, and a $6,000 Jacuzzi. The vice president of the owner's cargo company was also indicted for bribes to another Norfolk federal contract officer totaling over $75,000. In return for these gifts, the owner's company received over $640,000 in shipping contracts.

The owner faces up to five years in prison and $250,000 in fines. The two contract officers both pled guilty; the first has been sentenced to 44 months in prison, and the other awaits sentencing.

(Source: Hampton News, 10/25/05)

Employees Fail to Profit from Red Tape

Two workers at the Veterans Affair's Consolidated Mail Outpatient Pharmacy, which mails prescriptions to veterans, were charged with taking kickbacks for purchasing a product from a supplier at more than twice the normal price. The product? Red tape. The employees were charged with purchasing 100,000 rolls of the tape, which is stamped with the word "security" and is meant to deter tampering, at $6.95 a roll rather than its $2.50 retail value. In return, they received kickbacks of more than $1 per roll.

The duo will have plenty of time to appreciate the irony of their situation, as they face a sentence of 15 years in jail.

Reselling Commissary Goods Lands Two in Court

A scheme to resell military commissary batteries on the black market resulted in charges filed against a veteran and a Department of Defense employee. Investigators discovered that the veteran was bribing the employee to sell him large quantities of batteries from a commissary, which the veteran then resold at a profit to a distributor. During a one-year period, the employee sold the veteran $750,000 worth of batteries, which netted a $20,000 profit on the black market. The veteran kept $11,000 of the proceeds, and kicked back the remaining $9000 to the employee.

The veteran pled guilty to a misdemeanor charge of supplementing the salary of a Federal employee, and was sentenced to one year of probation. The employee was charged with bribery and taken to court. It is illegal for individuals to either pay or receive salary supplements for services performed by Government employees related to their Government duties.

Accepting Kickbacks Earns Contractor 11 Years

A federal investigation into bribery ended in three fraud convictions for the Chief of Plans, Requirements, and Acquisitions for the Defense Systems Agency at the Navy Ship Parts Control Center. The Department of Defense employee accepted $500,000 in cash in exchange for awarding $18.1 million in contracts to an information technology company. The investigation also uncovered a scheme by the employee, his brother, and his nephew to defraud an environmental remediation business by submitting phony invoices for more than $76,000. The employee was also convicted for lying about his wife's disability status to the Social Security Administration.

This trio of offenses earned the employee 11 years in federal prison, where he will have a family reunion with his brother and nephew as well as his daughter, who was convicted of making false statements to the grand jury. *(Source: York Daily Record, March 29, 2006)*

IRS Employee Goes to Jail for Accepting Gifts

In the course of collecting the debt from a construction company, an IRS Revenue Agent became friends with the owner. Such good friends, that the agent accepted free games of golf from the owner, as well as a number of free dinners at restaurants. Indeed, the owner and the agent were such pals that the owner presented the agent with a cashier's check for $14,900, which he subsequently used to purchase a car.

Unsurprisingly, the agent admitted that the gifts adversely affected his collection of the construction company's outstanding debt. The agent received three years in jail and six months of home confinement for an Unlawful Act of a Revenue Officer.

Postal Service Worker Faces Jail Time for Bribery

A U.S. Postal Service (USPS) employee responsible for receiving and awarding bids on USPS printing orders was arrested for trading Government contracts for cash. The employee funneled valuable contracts to the owner of a Washington D.C. printing business in exchange for payments of $11,575 to the employee's divorce lawyer. Over the course of the investigation, authorities uncovered four other printing companies that admitted paying bribes to the former USPS employee.

The printing business owner pled guilty to bribery, and faces up to two years in prison and a $250,000 fine. The USPS employee's case is pending in court.

Compensation for Representational Services from Non-Federal Sources (18 U.S.C. § 203-Type Violations)

Wanted: Employee Who Will Not Skip Meetings to Interview with Other Companies

An Army Brigadier General participated personally and substantially as an advocate and approval authority in the effort to increase funding on a task order with a Government contractor even while actively seeking employment with that company. His efforts did not rise to the level of "negotiating" employment so he did not violate the criminal prohibition of 18 U.S.C. §208, but was still in violation of C.F.R. 2635.604 when he took official action on behalf of a company with which he was seeking employment instead of disqualifying himself from the particular matter. He also extended official travel time and claimed unauthorized travel expenses in order to go to job interviews and participate in other job seeking activities to the point of actually excusing himself from official meetings. Finally, he charged unauthorized personal phone calls to the Government and ordered subordinates to run personal errands for him, including picking up his dry cleaning, driving him to the barber shop, and putting the license plates on his personal car (also directing them to use an official Government vehicle for these purposes). The General's behavior violated the Joint Ethics Regulation because he used Federal personnel, equipment, and duty time to conduct personal business. His official participation in a particular matter on behalf of a company with which he was seeking employment violated conflict of interest law. His other activities amounted to misuse of Government resources (his subordinates' time and the Government car) and improper gift acceptance (due to a failure to reimburse subordinates for expenditures such as mileage used when performing his personal services). As if that was not enough of an ethical rap sheet, he violated DoD Directive 7000.14-R when he decided to charge at least 15 of his TDY transactions to his personal credit card instead of his Government travel card so that he could receive bonus point or air miles on the card. The General was subject to Article 15 proceedings under the Uniform Code of Military Justice, fined $5,000, and directed to reimburse the Government $5,300 for the improper cell phone use and overpayment of TDY expenses. He was allowed to retire at his current grade, O-7.

Receipt of Income by Federal Employee Results in 18 U.S.C. 203 Violation

A former employee of the Department of Transportation was sentenced in the U.S. District Court for the Eastern District of Texas for receiving unauthorized compensation from a Government contractor for performing Government duties. The employee, in his capacity as a Supervisory Marine Surveyor for the Maritime Administration, accepted compensation from BGI Enterprise, Inc. for providing representational services in preparing a bid package for a $1 million U.S. Coast Guard contract to remove sunken barges from the Intracoastal Waterway in Texas.

The employee pled guilty to one count of violating 18 U.S.C. 203, and the Government dropped its charge of making false statements to the Government and failure to report the receipt of the unauthorized compensation on his annual financial disclosure form. The employee was sentenced to a one-year probation and ordered to pay a $2,500 fine.

Under this criminal statute, in general, Federal employees may not accept compensation for representing someone else before a Federal agency on particular matters in which the United States is a party.

INS Employee Accepts Illegal Payments

A clerical employee of the Immigration and Naturalization Service (INS) took money in exchange for assisting in processing INS employment authorization documents.

She pled guilty to a misdemeanor violation of 18 U.S.C. 203(a)(1), for receiving compensation for representational services rendered in a particular matter before a department or Agency of the United States. On December 12, 2000, she was sentenced to two years of probation and a $1,000 fine.

VA Employee Makes Improper Business Referrals

A decedent affairs clerk at a Veterans Affairs (VA) hospital acted as an agent of another employee at the VA hospital, who moonlighted at a nearby funeral home. The clerk referred VA officials to the funeral home where his coworker moonlighted for the handling of bodies abandoned at the VA hospital. The moonlighting employee paid the clerk for referrals. Payments totaled approximately $450.

The clerk pled guilty on October 13, 1999, to a misdemeanor violation of 18 U.S.C. 203(a)(1), for receiving compensation for representational services rendered in a particular matter before a department or Agency of the United States. On March 10, 2000, the moonlighting employee was sentenced to pay $25.

Congressional Staffer Accepts Cash in Return for Assistance with INS

A Congressional staff assistant for a member of Congress was assisting a constituent with filing an application to normalize the immigration status of the constituent's daughter. While doing so, he solicited and received money from the constituent in exchange for the preparation and filing of the application with the Immigration and Naturalization Service.

He was charged with violating 18 U.S.C. 203(a)(1)(B). On August 7, 1998, he pled guilty and on February 5, 1999, he was sentenced to three years' probation, 100 hours of community service, a $2,340 fine and $780 in restitution. Under this criminal statute, in general, Federal employees may not accept compensation for representing someone else before a Federal agency on particular matters in which the United States is a party.

IRS Employees Take Bribes To Ignore Tax Delinquency

Two employees of the Internal Revenue Service (IRS) and the two owners of a car rental business engaged in a scheme in which they conspired to improperly handle the company's delinquent tax debt. The company was experiencing serious financial problems and had substantial Federal employment tax delinquencies. The co-owners of the company met with an IRS employee who introduced them to another IRS employee. IRS employee number 2 told the co-owners how they could get their tax case transferred from the IRS office where it was pending to the IRS office where he was employed. At that point, he would permit the company to remain in business and pay a minimal amount of its tax deficiency. The co-owners agreed to a payment of $1,000 per month for this service. During this time period, the co-owners provided both IRS employees with free rental cars and paid vacations to Florida. IRS employee number 2 also invested money and acquired an interest in the company. In a separate scheme, IRS employee number 2 signed a one-year contract with a local levee board to perform an economic study. The contract called for the IRS employee to be paid $85 per hour; he received approximately $38,000 over the following year. At the same time, the levee board had tax disputes pending under the employee's supervision at the IRS. He did not disclose this fact to his supervisors at the IRS.

The rental car company owners each pled guilty to violating 18 U.S.C. 203, offering compensation to a Government employee for representational services rendered in a particular matter before a department or Agency of the United States. Owner number 1 received one year probation and a $250 fine. Owner number 2 was sentenced to five years of probation and $90,191 restitution. IRS employee number 1 pled guilty to violating 18 U.S.C. 201(b)(1)(A) (bribery) and was sentenced to five years of probation and a $3,000 fine. IRS employee number 2 pled guilty to violating 18 U.S.C. 208(a), taking official action in matters affecting a personal financial interest, as well as 18 U.S.C. 201(b)(2) (also bribery). He was sentenced to twelve months in jail, three years supervised release, and a $3,000 fine.

Congressional Staff Member Takes Payment to Help "Grease the Skids"

A Congressional staff member solicited $650 from a citizen who was seeking relief from the state's Office of Workman's Compensation. He told the citizen that the $650 would help "grease the skids" in getting her claim approved. The staff member specifically requested that money be provided in cash and arranged for it to be delivered outside of the Congresswoman's office where he worked. The citizen later reported the matter to the FBI – who introduced an undercover FBI agent who purported to have a worker's compensation claim. In tape-recorded conversations with the undercover agent, the staffer solicited $650 from the agent. The pay-off was videotaped. When interviewed several days later, he initially stated he never accepted money from a constituent. When shown a photo of the FBI agent, he stated that he had been offered money by her but had turned her down. When told that the person in the photo was an FBI agent, the staffer stated: "I guess I'm in a lot of trouble, aren't I?"

He was charged with violations of 18 U.S.C. 201 and 203 and pled guilty to one count of violating 18 U.S.C. 203. He received a sentence of probation and community service, and was ordered to pay restitution.

DOT Employee Sentenced for 18 U.S.C. 203 Violation

A former US Department of Transportation employee was sentenced in US District Court for receiving unauthorized compensation from a Government contractor for representing the contractor on a contract bid to the Government. The former official admitted that he assisted a DOT contractor in the preparation of a bid package for a $1 million Government contract. The judge sentenced the former employee to a year of probation and to pay a $2,500 fine.

Department of Labor Associate Deputy Under Secretary
Violates 18 U.S.C. 203

The Associate Deputy Under Secretary for International Labor Affairs at the Department of Labor was involved in an effort to promote low-income housing subsidized by the Mexican Government for low-paid Mexican workers living along certain sections of the United States-Mexican border. He was assigned the duty of pursuing arrangements for a low-cost housing project in 1991. The project was to be financed with private funds. He briefed the Deputy Under Secretary for International Labor Affairs on the progress of the project. During November 1991, he met with United States officials in Mexico City to discuss, among other things, private sector initiatives to construct low-cost housing along the United States-Mexican border. He met in Washington, D.C. and in Mexico City and other places with several real estate developers interested in low-cost housing along the border. He and the real estate developers met with Mexican banking and housing officials concerning the low-cost housing and the possibility that the project would be financed through a Mexican low-income financing authority. After several meetings, he told the real estate developers and the Mexican housing officials that he would not be able to participate in the joint venture that the real estate executives were forming due to his status as a Government employee. On July 22, 1992, the Under Secretary accepted the offer to work for the joint venture in dealings with the United States. He was offered 10 percent of the net profits generated by the project. The project involved the building of 6,000 condominiums and would generate about $10,000,000 in net profits. The anticipated total cost of the project was in excess of $120,000,000. The Under Secretary had an intermediary act on his behalf in signing a memorandum of agreement with the real estate developers. The Under Secretary, throughout the period in question, requested travel authorizations and submitted travel vouchers to the Government for travel to Mexico to work on the Mexican worker housing project

The Government charged that he agreed to accept compensation for representational services before the United States in relation to a particular matter, the housing project, in which the United States Department of Labor had a direct and substantial interest in violation of 18 U.S.C. 203(a) and 216(a)(2). The Government also claimed that the Under Secretary was acting as part of a conspiracy against the United States in violation of 18 U.S.C. 371. The Under Secretary pled guilty to the charges and was sentenced to probation for five years.

Immigration Consultant Offered Payment to INS Employee

An "immigration consultant" who assisted resident aliens with the process of obtaining INS travel papers offered compensation to an INS officer to speed up the application process.

He pled guilty to a misdemeanor violation of 18 U.S.C. 203(a)(2) on January 27, 1993, and was sentenced to one year probation, six months' home detention, and a $25 special assessment. The defendant was also prohibited from further working in the immigration consulting business.

Sergeant-at-Arms of the United States Senate Takes Free Flight to Hawaii After Recommending Contractor

The Sergeant-at-Arms is the chief purchasing agent for the Senate and in that capacity, he recommended that the Senate purchase and install a $219,000 AT&T telephone system for the U.S. Capitol Police. Three weeks later, he accepted a round-trip Washington-Honolulu airline ticket, valued at $2,700, from an AT&T employee.

He pled guilty on November 18, 1992 to one misdemeanor count of violating 18 U.S.C. 203 and was sentenced to one year of supervised probation and to pay full restitution of $2,700 and a $5,000 civil fine.

Citizen Gives Illegal Payoffs to IRS Employee

The defendant was audited by the Internal Revenue Service for excess deposits of income. He offered the IRS agent conducting the audit furniture, equipment, and cash if the agent would help him with his tax problems. The agent reported his offer to IRS internal security. Subsequent discussions between the citizen and the IRS agent, accompanied by payments of $240 and $200 in cash to the IRS agent, were monitored by IRS internal security.

The citizen pled guilty to a violation of 18 U.S.C. 203, for compensating a Government employee for representational services with respect to a particular matter in which the United States had a substantial interest. The defendant was given a sentence of probation.

Congressional Staff Member Pleads Guilty to 18 U.S.C. 203 Violation

The defendant was a staff assistant to a U.S. Congressman in a district office in Georgia whose responsibilities included handling constituent requests. The staffer demanded and received a payment of $300 from a businessman who was seeking a Federal grant to help him start up a business. The staffer also demanded a percentage of any grant money awarded to the businessman. He told the constituent that he would have to work nights and weekends on his own time to help the constituent and that the money was to compensate him for the work.

The staffer was indicted for personally seeking payment for official acts in violation of 18 U.S.C. 201(c) and for demanding compensation for representational services before the United States in violation of 18 U.S.C. 203. He pled guilty to the § 203 violation and received a sentence of probation.

And the Award Goes to…Our Sponsor!

The Director of the National Cancer Institute at the National Institutes of Health accepted a cash award from a grant recipient hospital. The doctor recused himself for a period of four weeks around the date of the award presentation from any dealings with the awarding hospital and noted the receipt of the award on his financial disclosure paperwork. Of course, this still leaves the question of whether the doctor was permitted by statute to accept gifts from the donor organization – which fell under the prohibited sources classification for purposes of the gift ban because of the doctor's potential influence over the selection of grant recipients. Congress has requested documentation on all NIH award recipients so stay tuned.

Conflicts of Interest (18 U.S.C. § 208-Type Violations)

Prime Contract, Turned Subcontractor, Turned Convict (Conflict of Interest)

The former Project Manager in charge of a prime contract in theater is now serving a 30 month prison sentence for criminal conflict of interest violations stemming from misconduct in the execution of his contract. The prime contractor was responsible for providing vehicle maintenance support to local units. In executing this contract, the Project Manager decided to try cheating the system by creating his own supply company and funneling subcontract opportunities to it. In executing this plan, the Project Manager awarded Blanket Purchase Agreements (BPAS), in excess of $10 million dollars, to his subcontracted supply company and marked up the price of his goods 100% or greater. A witness remarked that one example included charging the government $35 for filters with a fair market value of $10. When the Project Manager was promoted, his replacement discovered this misconduct and reported it. In addition to the 30 month prison sentence for criminal conflict of interest violations, the Project Manager was required to make restitution in excess of $2,300,000 and will be required to undergo two-years of supervised release following his prison sentence.

(Source: Department of Defense, Office of the Inspector General; 2015)

USAID Official Aids Himself

As Chief Financial Officer of the U.S. Agency for International Development (USAID), a former official helped draft a contract solicitation for a senior advisor—a position that he intended to apply for after he retired—and tailored the solicitation to his specific skills and experience. This is considered personal participation in a particular matter that has a direct and predictable effect on his financial interest. Thus, by violating the conflict of interest criminal statute, he was ordered to pay the Government a $30,000 penalty in settlement.

Documenting Misconduct

Jeffrey Davis, a former employee of the National Archives and Records Administration (NARA), faces a hefty penalty for engaging in a felony conflict of interest. Mr. Davis served as an Archives Technician at NARA, a position in which he assisted the public with requests for court documents maintained by NARA. He also owned and operated a company that charged its customers a fee for obtaining court records in addition to the fees charged by NARA. From September 2007 to October 2008, Davis used his official position at NARA to retrieve court documents for his company's customers. He also did not pay NARA the applicable fees associated with the company's customer requests for court records in order to conceal from NARA his affiliation with his company and to increase his company's profits.

Davis pled guilty to receiving payments from his company in connection with the retrieval of court records from NARA using his official position. He admitted such payments were an illegal supplementation of the salary paid by the government as compensation for his services as a NARA employee. Davis' sentencing is pending, but he faces the possibility of five years in prison and a $250,000 fine. It looks like his court records business has left him with a court record of his own.

One Happy Family Spends Time Together in Jail

A former programs director for the General Services Administration admitted to using his position at Fort Monmouth to award payments from the government to himself and his family. The former employee did this by awarding projects to two contractors who in turn hired the employee's personal business enterprise and his daughter as subcontractors. Over the course of three years, they received over $800,000 in fees from the government; the only catch, neither the employee's personal business nor his daughter actually performed any services for the government at all. Aside from the obvious fraud to which the former employee, his wife, and his daughter pled guilty, federal law also prohibits federal employees from making decisions concerning matters in which they or their family members have a personal financial interest. Even if the former GSA employee and his daughter had actually rendered the services that they billed for, the former employee would still have been in violation of federal law by awarding the projects to the contractors in the first place because his own financial interests were involved. The former GSA employee and his family were ordered to pay over $800,000 in restitution, and they each received prison sentences ranging from 12 to 46 months.

Moonlighting for Contractor Results in Employee Termination

A contract manager at a Tennessee Valley Authority (TVA) power plant in Kentucky found himself out two jobs after investigators learned that he had been moonlighting for the same contractor he was overseeing. As part of his responsibilities with TVA, the contract manager reviewed contractor bids and oversaw contract performance. The manager accepted a job with one of TVA's contractors as a part-time supervisor, and worked for the contractor in Oklahoma and Indiana on his days off and vacation days.

Even though the manager's actions did not result in any identified financial loss, he was terminated from TVA and prosecuted for a violation of 18 U.S.C. 208. He pled guilty and was sentenced to probation and a $1,000 fine.

This criminal statute prohibits personnel from participating in official actions (such as reviewing contractor bids) that affect their employer, even if they work for that employer only part time.

Awarding Contracts to Friend Earns Employee Five Years of Probation

Investigators quickly short-circuited the plans of a NASA employee to cash in on an agency electrical services contract. The employee worked as a communications specialist at Langley Research Center (LaRS), and was responsible for reviewing and approving work done on a project to install new "telecommunications closets" in LaRS. The employee recommended that the main project contactor hire a certain subcontractor, which coincidentally was wholly owned and operated by the employee's friend. The prime contractor agreed. The subcontractor completed the work, and subsequently bid on another subcontract. Upon receiving this second contract, the subcontractor covertly hired another company to complete the work; this company was wholly owned and operated by the NASA employee himself. At this point, tipsters notified investigators, who found that the scam had netted the pair over $40,000.

The employee pled guilty to violating the conflict of interest statute, and was sentenced to five years of probation and a $5,000 fine. This conflict of interest statute prohibits personnel from participating in official actions (including merely making a recommendation) that affect their financial interests.

Awarding Contracts to Spouse Earns Couple One Year in Prison

A former Department of the Treasury employee and her husband were sentenced to a year in prison for a scheme to funnel contracts to companies they personally controlled. The employee, who served as an Employee Development Specialist, was responsible for determining the training needs of Treasury employees and procuring private training services. Investigators discovered that over the course of two years, the employee had awarded 105 training contracts valued at more than $139,600 to companies owned by her husband.

The employee pled guilty to several charges, including violations of 18 U.S.C. 208, participating personally and substantially in matters in which she or her spouse had a financial interest. She was sentenced to a year of prison and three years of supervised release, and was ordered to pay $54,500 in restitution. Her husband also pled guilty to several charges, including wire fraud and conspiracy, and received the same sentence as his wife.

Awarding Contracts to Spouse II

A contracting officer for the General Services Administration (GSA) wound up in Federal court after funneling contracts to her husband's employer. Investigators discovered that the officer had directed over $11.5 million to the company that employed her husband over the span of 15 months, all in the form of GSA purchases of food preparation and serving equipment items. As a result of these purchases, the officer's husband received raises and a Jaguar from his employer.

The officer pled guilty to violating conflict of interest laws, and was sentenced to 180 days of home confinement and five years of probation. She additionally was ordered to pay $161,000 in restitution.

Awarding Contracts to Spouse III

The head of the Law Enforcement Coordinating Committee Program at the U.S. Attorney's Office for the Middle District of Louisiana discovered he had done his job too well when he was arrested and prosecuted for violating conflict of interest laws. Authorities learned that the employee, who was responsible for arranging training seminars that would foster cooperation with state and local law enforcement, had funneled seminar contracts to a certain company; this company then subcontracted to a company owned by the employee's wife. This scheme had funneled $55,000 to the employee's wife, and the company had kicked back $20,000 directly to the employee himself.

The employee pled guilty to violating 18 U.S.C. 208, participating personally and substantially in a matter in which he or his spouse had a financial interest, and was sentenced to three years of probation, 200 hours of community service, and a $5,000 fine.

And the Band Played On...While the Ship Sank Around Them

An Assistant Secretary of Telecommunications and Information within the Department of Commerce spoke with ethics officers about a small dinner party she was having at her home but neglected to mention: a) the party was for between 60 and 80 people and b) it was paid for by companies she was responsible for regulating. Although the ethics officers found her to be in violation of the department's regulations, the Justice Department elected not to press criminal charges.

Watch Promoting Your Business on Government Time!

The Facts: A Senior Advisor to the State Department had an interest in a business that planned to develop a theme park in the Middle East. No problem there. But the Advisor, in his official position, recommended to other State Department officials that the State Department support the enterprise. That violated the law. After a guilty plea, he was sentenced to a year of probation and ordered to perform 25 hours community service and to pay a $20,000 fine. (Source: *Federal Ethics Report*, Dec. 2000.)

The Law: 18 U.S.C. § 208 (2003) forbids any employee of the executive branch of the Federal Government from recommending in his or her official position any matter in which he or she has a financial interest. The penalty for violating this law could be a fine, a prison sentence for up to one year, or both—unless the violation is found to be "willful," in which case the maximum prison sentence increases to 5 years (*see* 18 U.S.C. § 216 (2003)).

Helping to Contract with a Potential Employer — A Bad Idea

The Facts: A U.S. State Department official was negotiating an employment contract with a private employer when he recommended in his official capacity that the Department of Defense (DoD) enter into a contract with the same company. The aim of the contract: to provide equipment and transportation to help recover the remains of U.S. servicemen who were missing in action during the Korean War. Relying upon the official's recommendation, DoD contracted with that company for $717,000. Unfortunately, the official's recommendation to contract with a company with whom he was negotiating employment violated the law. On January 10, 2002, the State Department official was sentenced to three years' probation and ordered to pay a $5,000 fine. (Source: *Federal Ethics Report*, Feb. 2002.)

The Law: With some exceptions, 18 U.S.C. § 208 (2003) forbids any officer or employee of the executive branch from participating "personally and substantially" in his or her official capacity in a contract, controversy, "or other particular matter" in which he or she, or any person or organization with whom he is she is negotiating employment, has a financial interest. Anyone violating this law "shall be imprisoned for not more than one year," fined, or both (*see* 18 U.S.C. § 216). By making a recommendation on a contract involving a company with which he was negotiating employment, the official in this case violated the law.

Judge Imposes Steep Prison Sentence in Conflict of Interest Case

A former employee of the District of Columbia Government was sentenced in the U.S. District Court for the District of Columbia for overseeing contracts involving an individual with whom he was financially involved. The former employee served as chief of the day programs branch of the D.C. Mental Retardation and Developmental Disabilities Administration. This Administration placed mentally retarded adults in non-residential day programs. The former employee supervised the assignment of mentally retarded adults to day programs and administered the rules governing these programs. During this time, the former employee assisted a woman in starting up a day treatment program for mentally retarded adults. The former employee made loans to the woman and referred clients to her. Thus, the former employee had a financial relationship with the woman. The former employee was no longer impartial since he had a financial interest in seeing her succeed so his loan could be paid back. In addition, as part of his D.C. Government duties, he oversaw the supervision of her company. When she would pay back a portion of the loan, she would also pay him additional monies.

The jury found the former employee guilty of conspiracy and of violation of the conflict-of-interest law. Particularly because of the involvement of a vulnerable victim (the mentally retarded individuals in the day program), the judge sentenced the former employee to 46 months in prison, followed by 3 years of supervised release to include 100 hours of community service. The judge also ordered the former employee to pay a $25,000 fine.

Federal conflict of interest statutes prohibit employees from taking official action in particular matters in which they have a financial interest.

**Federal Employee Convicted of Conflict of Interest Violation
While Searching for New Job**

Job-hunting efforts by a former Commerce Department Inspector General (IG) turned up a Federal conviction for a conflict of interest instead of a job. As part of the former IG's official duties, he reviewed the performance of a certain company, which had contracted with the Commerce Department to update automated weather forecasting systems. At the same time that he was performing these oversight duties, the former official began negotiating employment with the same company.

A Federal criminal statute, 18 U.S.C. 208, prohibits Federal employees from officially working on particular matters that have a direct and predictable effect on an organization with which they are negotiating prospective employment. The former IG's review of the company's performance on the Commerce Department contract violated this statute. This is the same statute that bars Federal employees from taking official action on matters that affect their own financial interests or those of their spouses or children.

CIA Conflict of Interest

A CIA employee paid $48,000 to settle a complaint brought by the Department of Justice that the employee had participated in official matters in which his spouse had a financial interest. The employee had served as the Contracting Officer Technical Representative (COTR) on certain contracts between his agency and a private corporation, where his wife worked. The contracts involved millions of dollars awarded to the corporation. Although the employee's wife did not work on the same contracts as the employee, she received stock options for the purchase of the corporation's stock that were affected by the corporation's profits from the contracts her husband had worked on.

A criminal statute, 18 U.S.C. 208, prohibits employees from participating personally and substantially in matters that have a direct and predictable effect on their own financial interests or those of their spouses, minor children, or organizations in which they are employed. In this case, the employee's involvement in the corporation's contracts affected the profitability of the corporation, which was passed on to the employee's wife through her stock options.

Former Postmaster General Pays Settlement
to End Conflict of Interest Investigation

A former Postmaster General of the United States agreed to pay a $27,550 settlement to end a complaint brought by the Department of Justice pertaining to a conflict of interest involving the official's holdings in a soft drink company. The complaint arose while the Postal Service was exploring a potential strategic alliance between the Postal Service and the soft drink company. T he Postal Service Board of Governors had the authority to approve the strategic alliance, and the Postmaster General's role was to advise the Board of Governors with regard to their consideration of strategic alliances. The Postmaster General rendered advice to the Board even though he owned shares of stock in the soft drink company and therefore had a personal financial interest in the decision.

The Postmaster General was charged specifically with violating 18 U.S.C. 208, a criminal statute that prohibits an employee from participating personally and substantially, as a Government official, in a particular matter in which he or she has a financial interest.

High-Ranking Government Official Agrees to Conflict of Interest Settlement

A high-ranking Government official was charged with violating 18 U.S.C. 208, which governs official acts affecting a personal financial interest. The Federal employee, an Assistant to the President for National Security Affairs, was investigated for holding stock in certain petroleum companies while serving as the Deputy Assistant to the President for National Security Affairs. The employee was advised by the National Security Council Legal Adviser to divest his shares of his family's petroleum and other energy-producing stocks to avoid any conflict of interest. During the time the employee was told to divest his stocks, he was involved in his official capacity in matters that may have had a direct and predictable effect on the petroleum company.

The official agreed to pay the Department of the Treasury $23,043, which represented the increased value of the stocks, to settle the matter.

D.C. Public Library Director Sentenced for Travel Reimbursement Scheme

The former director of the District of Columbia Public Library was convicted for fraudulent activities involving Government cash advances and reimbursement payments. At the time, the director was serving as both the head of the D.C. Public Library and the president of a trade organization, the American Library Association. The director took cash advances from D.C. Public Library funds to pay for expenses incurred in his role as president of the American Library Association. He then asked the trade organization to reimburse him by sending checks directly to his home address. In this manner, the library director deposited over $24,000 into his personal bank account. Subsequently, the director failed to reimburse the D.C. Public Library account for the cash advances.

In September 1998, a judge ordered the former director to pay back the $24,000 owed to the D.C. Library, plus an additional $16,860 owed for back Federal income taxes. He was sentenced to five months of home detention, to be followed by two years of probation for violation of 18 U.S.C. 208, a conflicts of interest criminal statute.

Former Federal Bureau of Investigation (FBI) Agent Violates Conflict of Interest Statute

A former FBI agent pled guilty to violating 18 U.S.C. 208, which prohibits Federal employees from participating in official acts in which they have a personal financial interest. The agent's job responsibilities included researching and testing the use of pepper spray for the FBI, which resulted in contact with the manufacturers of one particular type of pepper spray. The agent subsequently recommended this pepper spray, and in return, received $57,500 in payments from the manufacturer. Following the agent's recommendation, the FBI approved the use of the pepper spray for its agents, resulting in a large purchase from the manufacturer. Additionally, as a result of the FBI agent's research and recommendation, other law enforcement agencies nationwide began to use the pepper spray produced by the manufacturer.

The former agent was sentenced to two months imprisonment followed by three years of supervised release for his violation of 18 U.S.C. 208. This statute bars Federal employees from officially participating (in this case, even making a recommendation) in particular matters (in this case, a contract to buy pepper spray) that have a direct and predictable effect on the employee's financial interests or those of the employee's spouse or minor children.

Army Employee Sentenced for Conflicts of Interest

A civilian employee of the U.S. Army pleaded guilty to violation of the conflicts of interest statute (18 U.S.C. 208) in Federal Court and was sentenced to one year probation and a $1,000 fine. The employee had participated in the awarding and administration of contracts involving a company in which the employee owned stock, thereby participating personally and substantially as a Government employee in matters that affected his financial interests. The employee, who filed financial disclosure statements (OGE Form 450), had also failed to disclose his financial interest in the company.

47

Chief Financial Officer and Chief Information Officer of the United States Department of Education Violates 18 U.S.C. 208

While the official held the above titles at the Department of Education, his wife owned 600 shares of Compaq computer stock that she had inherited from her mother. During this period, the official was involved in his official capacity in issues concerning Compaq computers. The Government contended that the official violated 18 U.S.C. 208, for participating personally and substantially as a Government officer in a particular matter in which, to his knowledge, he and/or his spouse has a financial interest.

Pursuant to a civil settlement, the official paid the Government $20,000, and the Government released him from its claims.

Chief of Staff at the Department of Veterans Affairs Medical Center in Kansas City, Engages in Conflict of Interest

During the same time the Chief of Staff was employed by the Department of Veterans Affairs Medical Center, he was also employed as a physician by the University of Kansas Medical Center in Kansas City, Kansas. Subsequently, the Chief of Staff in his official capacity approved a contract for cardiocath services to the Department of Veterans Affairs Medical Center by the University of Kansas Medical Center.

On March 8, 2000, the Chief of Staff pled guilty to a misdemeanor violation of 18 U.S.C. 208, which bars employees from taking official action in matters affecting their personal financial interests. On August 7, 2000, he was sentenced to pay a $250 fine and a special assessment of $25.

Internal Revenue Service (IRS) Revenue/Settlement Officer Prosecuted UP 18 U.S.C. 208

An IRS employee was assigned to a certain IRS collection matter, which gave him inside information concerning a proposed stock exchange. After his role in the case was substantially over, the employee purchased approximately $2,000 in the stock subject to the proposed exchange based in part on information he had learned during the course of his duties as a Revenue Officer. After the stock purchase, the IRS employee had on several occasions, minor contact with the parties before the IRS. He eventually went to his supervisor, disclosed his interest in the stock, and was removed from further participation in the case. The IRS employee lost money on the stock transaction.

The IRS employee was prosecuted pursuant to 18 U.S.C. 208 for participating personally and substantially as a Government officer or employee in a particular matter in which, to his knowledge, he had a financial interest, and 18 U.S.C. 216(a)(1). The employee was placed on pretrial diversion for six months on the condition that he resign from the IRS and perform 120 hours of community service.

District Conservationist at Department of Agriculture's National Resources Conservation Service Sentenced for Conflict of Interest

The NRCS employee was the Government's technical representative on a USDA soil and water conservation program that was implemented through a State of North Carolina program called NCACSP (North Carolina Agricultural Cost Share Program). Under the NCACSP program, local landowners can receive funding to reduce agricultural pollution. The NRCS employee, in his position as a district conservationist, approved a contract whereby a business venture owned by his spouse sold filter fabric to landowners through the NCACSP program.

The NRCS employee was charged with a felony count of violating 18 U.S.C. 2, aiding and abetting, and 18 U.S.C. 208, for participating personally and substantially as a Government employee in a particular matter, in which, to his knowledge, his spouse has a financial interest. Further, in his position as a district conservationist, he approved a contract between the NCACSP and a cattle operation in which he and his spouse were partners. Additionally, he approved a contract for fence construction between the NCACSP and a third party. This contract resulted in payments that were transferred to a partnership consisting of the NRCS employee, his spouse, and the third party. The NRCS employee was charged with two additional felony counts of violating 18 U.S.C. 208, for participating personally and substantially as a Government employee in a particular matter, in which, to his knowledge, he, his spouse, and general partner have a financial interest. A jury convicted the NRCS employee on all counts. He was sentenced by the court to one year of probation.

A Contracting Officer for the Department of the Army at Fort Jackson Settles Conflict of Interest Allegation

Sometime prior to November 1995, the contracting officer began a relationship with a foreman for a Government contractor. The foreman subsequently started his own company and began bidding on Government contracts at Fort Jackson. In November 1995, the former Government contracting officer assumed the title of project manager at the new company and performed various duties for the former foreman without monetary compensation. On April 9, 1996, the contracting officer approved and certified for payment an invoice submitted by the company. She continued her employment relationship with the company until June 1996. However, she submitted a written statement to the Director of Contracting at Fort Jackson attesting that her association with the company ended in March 1996.

The former contracting officer was indicted on December 3, 1997 for violating 18 U.S.C. 208, taking official action in matters affecting an employee's personal financial interest. She signed a Pretrial Diversion Agreement which requires that she complete 50 hours of community service.

Assistant United States Attorney (AUSA) Convicted on Conflict of Interest and Fraud

The AUSA for the Central District of California was indicted after it was discovered that on numerous occasions he had made favorable recommendations to the court, the probation office, and other prosecuting offices on behalf of cooperating witnesses and defendants in exchange for hundreds of thousands of dollars. The AUSA had, for example, accepted $98,000 from one cooperating witness who had previously been convicted in the Northern District of Texas and on whose behalf the AUSA had argued for leniency at the sentencing hearing. In addition, he had used his official position to secure entry into the United States of several foreign nationals whom he believed would make substantial investments in a company in which he and his wife had a controlling financial interest. Once the foreign nationals entered the United States, two Iranian companies with which they were affiliated loaned a total of $860,000 to the AUSA's company.

The AUSA pled guilty to one felony conflict of interest count, 18 U.S.C. 208, and two counts of wire fraud, in violation of 18 U.S.C. 1343 and 1346. He was fined $7,500 and sentenced to two years in prison plus three years of supervised release.

Patrick Air Force Base Engineer Violates Conflict of Interest Statute

An engineer in the Contracts Department at Patrick Air Force Base started a business, along with former military personnel and former Government employees, which submitted a bid to the base. The engineer, in his official capacity, provided the technical evaluations on the bid. Through the bidding process, the company was awarded the contract.

The engineer was charged with participating personally and substantially in a particular matter in which he had a financial interest, in violation of 18 U.S.C. 208. Pursuant to 18 U.S.C. 216(a)(1), he pled guilty to a misdemeanor violation of section 208 and was sentenced to nine months' probation and fined $2,500.

Federal Aviation Administration (FAA) Employee Guilty of Violating 18 U.S.C. 208

The FAA employee reviewed the applications of aircraft component manufacturers. He was the FAA representative on a flight test of a Ground Proximity Warning System (GPWS) manufactured by a certain corporation. In the course of his duties for the FAA, the employee obtained access to proprietary information submitted to the FAA by the GPWS manufacturer. At the same time, the FAA employee was developing and marketing his own GPWS for sale to the public.

The FAA employee was charged with a violation of 18 U.S.C. 208 due to the fact that he participated personally and substantially in the FAA's test flight of a GPWS while developing his own GPWS; he pled guilty and was sentenced to three years of probation.

CIA Employee Violates Conflict of Interest Statute

A Central Intelligence Agency Contracting Officer's Technical Representative (COTR) pled guilty to a violation of 18 U.S.C. 208 after investigators discovered that he had used his Government position to secure employment for a friend who owed him money. The employee's duties as a COTR included the technical supervision of two Government contracts with a particular company through which the Government funded a classified program. The employee used his position as a COTR to cause the company to hire one of his friends as a consultant to the program. The friend owed a substantial sum of money to the employee and his wife and did not have the financial means to repay them. At no time did the employee disclose to the Government or the company that the friend owed him or his wife money. The Government charged that, under these circumstances, the COTR had a financial interest in the company's decision to enter into a consulting agreement with the friend and that he violated 18 U.S.C. 208 by participating in that decision.

The COTR pled guilty to a felony violation of section 208. He also pled guilty to a charge of possession of child pornography obtained through unauthorized personal use of a Government-furnished computer. He received three years supervised release and was ordered to pay a $4,000 fine.

Computer-Aided Navigation Leaves Retired Captain Lost at Sea

A Coast Guard Captain working on the integration of legacy navigation systems with GPS spoke with a government contractor assigned to the project about post-retirement work. Once retired, the captain made recommendations concerning purchases to his former colleagues still wearing Coast Guard uniforms – purchases that directly benefited the captain in his new role as consultant. The government maintained that the captain violated 18 U.S.C. § 208(a), by negotiating for future employment with a contractor he dealt with in his active duty capacity and 18 U.S.C. § 207 (a)(1), by attempting to influence government personnel on a project over which he had exercised considerable responsibility. The Government settled with the captain for $25,000.

Conflict of Interest Results in $10,000 Fine

A Navy Construction Representative overseeing a company's two construction contracts with the Navy secured employment to subcontract the same projects he was supposedly inspecting, splitting the proceeds with an equally unscrupulous employee of the company. He pled guilty to one count of violating 18 U.S.C. § 208 (barring an employee from taking official action in matters affecting certain personal or organizational financial interests) and one count of violating 41 U.S.C. § 53, the Anti-Kickback Act of 1986. His get-rich-quick scheme cost him six years' probation, six months home detention, 100 hours of community service, and a $10,000 fine.

Agricultural Economist and Wife Violate 18 U.S.C. 208 in Visa Scam

A Department of Agriculture agricultural economist found himself facing jail time for his decision to attempt to exploit his Government position. The economist was put in charge of a Department program to bring together U.S. and Chinese agriculture experts. Instead, the economist forged documents, with the assistance of his wife, to extort $82,000 from nearly 100 Chinese nationals seeking entry to the United States. While the economist's case is still pending, his wife pled guilty to one count of aiding and abetting an unlawful conflict of interest in violation of 18 U.S.C. §§ 208 and 2. She received two years of probation and 100 hours of community service.

Consultant's Attempted Bribery Garners $1000 Fine

A consultant in the office of the District of Columbia Chief Technology Officer ended up in court after soliciting kickbacks from a private company. The consultant was tasked with awarding contracts to information technology companies, and decided to go back to a company he had recently approved and demand a cut of their profits. Unhappily for him, the company went to the authorities instead. The consultant pled guilty to one count of violating 18 U.S.C. § 208 (a), taking official action in matters affecting an employee's personal financial interest, and was sentenced to a year of probation and a $1000 fine.

Attempted Bribery of Immigration Official Nets a Year of Probation

An applicant for U.S. citizenship slid $200 in an unmarked envelope across to an Adjudication Officer during his interview, hoping for a favorable outcome. He got a year of probation instead.

Contractors and Army Officer Face Five Years for Conflict of Interest

A raid of an Army Colonel's residence revealed evidence that led to charges for the officer as well as two employees of a Maryland military contractor. The officer supervised solicitation, award, and oversight of more than 17,000 military contracts in Korea. Upon learning that the officer was considering retirement, two military contractors contacted him regarding his potential employment at the contractors' company. Over the course of the next six months, the officer and the contractors had lengthy discussions regarding the possible job offer.

The negotiations involved a trip to company headquarters as well as at least seven dinners at expensive restaurants, all paid for by the company.

During this time period, the officer did not recuse himself from matters involving the company. In fact, the officer on one occasion overruled the decision of technical experts who recommended awarding a contract to a different company, and instead recommended the contractors' company. On another occasion, the officer told another contractor that if he wished to participate in the program in the future, he should bid as a subcontractor to the first contractors' company. The contractors' internal emails advocating the officer's hiring noted that "[h]is expectations are high but his value has been proved."

Tips from a member of the officer's command led to an interagency investigation which uncovered egregious bribe-taking to the tune of more than $700,000 (much of which was found hidden in bundles of cash under the officer's mattress) – in addition to the illegal negotiations with the contractors. These bribes had resulted in nearly $25 million in contracts being illegally rewarded to companies for building facilities and providing security guards at military installations in Korea.

The officer pled guilty to charges of conspiracy and bribery, and was sentenced to 54 months in prison followed by three years of supervised release. He was also assessed a $10,000 fine, was stripped of rank, and will receive no retirement pay. The two contractors face five years in prison and a $250,000 fine.

Employee Fined $13,000 for Conflict of Interest

A Supervisory Acquisition Management Specialist at Wright-Patterson Air Force Base was indicted for participating in employment negotiations with a company while he simultaneously worked on contracts involving that company. As part of the employee's job responsibilities, he provided a bidder on a Government contract with advice and made recommendations related to the bidding process. However, at the same time, the employee was in employment negotiations with one of the bidder's subcontractors, and was well aware of the subcontractor's interest in the bidder's success.

The employee pled guilty to violating the conflict of interest statute that prohibits an individual from engaging in employment negotiations with a company while simultaneously participating in an official capacity on a Government contract with the company.

The employee was sentenced to one year of probation and ordered to pay $12,000 in restitution and a $1,000 fine.

Conflict of Interest Nets Employee $900 Fine

When determining which company should receive a contract to produce a video on Y2K issues for the Department of Commerce, a producer/director in the Office of Public Affairs settled on a small production company that specialized in voiceover work. There was only one small problem—the company was owned by the employee and his wife. The Department of Commerce eventually paid the company over $10,000 for their work, earning the employee and his wife a profit of over $1000.

Unfortunately for the employee, his fifteen minutes of fame were cut short by a District Court Judge, who sentenced him to one year of probation, 100 hours of community service, and a $900 fine. The employee was found guilty of violating 18 U.S.C. 208(a), which bars employees from participating personally and substantially in a matter in which they have a financial interest.

Employee Fined $1000 for Conflict of Interest

Funneling contracts to friends certainly did not pay off for the Senior Development Officer of the International Broadcasting Bureau (IBB). The officer was responsible for developing and securing funding for revenue-producing projects for the IBB, an independent agency affiliated with the State Department. When determining which company should receive an $85,000 grant to train affiliate radio stations in Uganda, the officer selected a business owned by his friend. In return for this generosity, his friend obligingly selected a subcontractor near and dear to the officer's heart – a company owned and managed by the officer and his wife. In order to fulfill the $15,000 contract, the officer managed to convince IBB to fly him to Uganda with government funds as part of his "official duties." However, IBB soon discovered the officer's relationship with the subcontracting company.

For his violation of 18 U.S.C. 208, which forbids employees from participating personally and substantially in a matter in which they have a financial interest, the officer earned three years of probation, 50 hours community service, a $1000 fine, and was required to pay over $15,000 in restitution.

Conflict of Interest Results in Jail Time for Acquisitions Executive

A former senior Air Force official found herself in Federal prison after her violation of conflicts-of-interest statutes. The official engaged in job negotiations with a private company while still employed by the Air Force as the chief negotiator for a $23 billion leasing plan with that company. While the official did eventually recuse herself from participation in decisions involving the company, her recusal came three months after the beginning of her negotiations.

The official began negotiations with the company through encrypted e-mails sent by her daughter, who was an employee of the company; her daughter set up a secret meeting between the official and company executives. At the start of the meeting, the official informed the executives that she was still participating personally and substantially on matters involving the company; however, both parties elected to continue the meeting and to simply keep it a secret. The negotiations continued for several more months, all while the official was still participating personally and substantially in decisions, approvals, and advice in matters in which the company had a financial interest. After the official finally submitted her letter disqualifying herself from working on matters involving the company, investigators began scrutinizing the timeline of her story. The official lied repeatedly to investigators as to the start date of her employment negotiations, collaborating with the company executives to match stories.

The former official pled guilty in Federal court, and was sentenced to nine months in prison and seven months either in a halfway house or under home detention. The company executive faces a jail term of no more than six months under Federal sentencing guidelines.

Federal Procurement law specifically forbids a company or its executives from making any offer or promise of future employment to a Federal procurement officer. Likewise, procurement officers are prohibited from discussing employment so long as they oversee matters involving that company.

Credit Card Abuse

Don't Syphon the Government Coffers

A number of Federal employees in recent months have been caught using their government credit cards for personal use. A reportedly $2.4 million problem since 2010, over 260 cases of government employee misuse have been adjudicated in that time. With roughly 200,000 vehicles in federal government service, that equates to about $12 per vehicle.

A handful of adjudicated cases from April to September 2014 shed light as to the repercussions for this conduct. First, a Department of Homeland Security contractor was accused of government credit card misuse and pled guilty in May to using a number of GSA credit cards to fuel his vehicle. His sentencing included a six month jail sentence, one year of probation, debarment from government service for three years, and $3,920 in restitution. Another federal employee, employed by the Navy, pled guilty to similar offenses and received five months in jail, a bad-conduct discharge, and was required to pay $20,000 in restitution. Bottom Line: Don't syphon gas—literally and figuratively.

(Source: The Washington Post; published 27 Feb 2015)

Furlough No Defense to Misuse of Government Credit Card

When the Government shut down occurred nearly two years ago, a Federal employee decided to use his Government credit card to purchase nearly $12,000 worth of groceries, hotel rooms, cable TV and ferry rides. The employee, from the Department of Housing and Urban Development (HUD), was not immediately caught for misuse of the card because the supervisors overseeing the use of the Government credit card were also on furlough. Nevertheless, sometime after the furlough, the misuse was detected. The HUD employee was placed on administrative leave until April 2014, and is now in a court-ordered drug rehabilitation program. The employee is required to pay full restitution.

(Source: The Washington Post: published 24 July 2015)

Agency Credit Card Swindler 2

A Drug Enforcement Administration manager admitted to opening and using dozens of government credit cards under fake employee aliases. In pleading guilty, the manager admitted to having opened 32 fake credit cards to withdraw $114,000 in cash from ATMs. This conduct spanned over three years. The manager had duties permitting her authority to approve and issue credit cards for agency employees. Wire fraud, the offense the employee pled guilty to, carries a maximum penalty of 20 years imprisonment and a $250,000 fine. As part of her plea arrangement, however, a three year jail sentence is expected and she will be required to pay full restitution for the withdrawals.

(Source: The Washington Post; published 17 Apr 2015)

Government Travel Cards Are Not a Blank Check

An officer has been reprimanded for misuse of his Government Travel Card (GTC). According to DoD regulations, GTCs are only to be used for costs related to official government travel and not personal, family, or household purposes unrelated to official travel. According to witnesses and the officer's own admission, he knowingly misused his card, and allowed his wife to misuse it as well, in purchasing groceries, toys, and household items. These "extras" were purchases in part, per the officer's sworn statements, because he had been taking care of his sickly mother. This misconduct occurred despite having recently received remedial GTC training in 2013 after purchasing dinner for his future boss and family. Upon further investigation, other non-travel related purchases were discovered to have been made after this training as well. For his failure to safeguard and use his GTC appropriately, the officer was served with a General Officer Memorandum of Reprimand.

(Source: Department of Defense, Office of the Inspector General; 2015)

Government Employees Double Down on Taxpayer-Funded Gambling

Two Government employees used their government-issued credit cards to fund their gambling and bowling binge, to the tune of almost $35,000. Unfortunately, gambling was just not enough. One of the employees, a manager, racked up an additional $13,000 in expenses to cover car rentals for personal use. In the end, approximately $47,000 of the tax payer's money bankrolled the employees' fun and games. The manager, spending a total of $45,000, repaid the debt to the Government and took an early retirement. The other employee, spending a total of $2,400, repaid the debt to the Government and was fired.

Sporting Goods Scam Steals from Uncle Sam

It seemed like the perfect scam: Owners of a sporting goods store near a military installation allowed service-members to charge personal items on government purchase cards (GPC). Service-members would overcharge the cards and then split the extra cash between themselves and the store owners. One unlucky E-6 was caught when he charged $1950 on a GPC and pocketed $850, which he used to buy a number of sporting goods. The perfect scam didn't work out so well for the E-6. He was convicted in a court martial, reduced to E-1, given 18 months confinement, and given a bad conduct discharge.

Pin-Heads Ignore Government Purchase Card Procedures

The Manager of an Army Bowling Pro Shop received factory rebates for the bowling products he purchased for the shop using a Government credit card. Government Purchase Card procedures stipulate that cardholders should take advantage of any rebates offered, whether cash or merchandise, and that manufacturer and retailer rebates should be made payable to the appropriate Government agency. The Manager purchased property for the shop, a MWR entity, on a Government contract; therefore, the rebates were the property of DoD and should have been turned in to the agency's financial officer. Instead, the Manager kept the rebates, which were in the form of Best Buy gift cards, for his personal use. He was even heard bragging about all of the free stuff he would be able to buy. Furthermore, he improperly lent his Government impact card to another civilian bowling facility employee in violation of Government Purchase Card standard operating procedure which requires that only the named individual on the card may use it for official purposes in compliance with agency accounts. This employee kept the cash and gift card rebates he received from using the Manager's card; failing to provide them to the MWR finance officer and resulting in a $230 cost loss for the Government. These actions constitute larceny and improper use of a Government purchase card. The Manager resigned in lieu of further disciplinary action. The employee also resigned.

Electronics Scam Lands Sailor in Hot Water

An active duty Navy sailor and authorized Government purchase card user noticed one day that some of the items she had purchased for her Command were missing from the warehouse. She decided to go ahead and repurchase the items to "prevent any of her shipmates from getting in trouble for stealing Government property." This incident seemed to give the sailor an idea because about two years later she decided to try to use her Government purchase card to conduct widespread theft. Ever cautious, she first conducted a few "test runs" by purchasing items for her personal use on her Government card. The misuse went undetected so the sailor joined with a co-conspirator to discuss even bigger plans. They decided to buy laptop computers and plasma televisions on the sailor's Government card and to re-sell them for personal profit. Navy auditors discovered the scheme and determined that the sailor and her co-conspirator had defrauded the Government out of $363,243. The sailor had used her Government card to purchase 162 notebook computers, 65 big screen televisions, 22 digital cameras, GPS devices, camcorders, computer monitors, and home theater systems. Her efforts to prevent her shipmates from getting into trouble and her subsequent emulation of the local cut-rate electronic retailer led the sailor to plead guilty to one count of theft of Government property in violation of 18 U.S.C. §641. She is scheduled for sentencing in August 2008.

Stealing Isn't Only Way to Misuse a Government Issued Credit Card

A U.S. Postal Service employee received a Government Issued Credit Card (GICC) through Citibank to cover relocation costs. In receiving the GICC, the employee signed a contract with Citibank stating he would pay the entire balance of the credit card within 25 days of the billing statement closing date. He also agreed with the U.S.P.S. to pay the balance on time regardless of whether or not he had received reimbursement. The employee accrued a balance of over $6,000 on the account, but did not make an initial payment on the balance until four months after the due date, and did not pay off the entire balance until 10 months after the due date. The employee procrastinated in requesting reimbursement and then he waited six weeks before depositing the reimbursement check and making a payment toward the balance on the credit card. The employee also retained a portion of the reimbursement funds for himself, leaving a balance on the card for six more months. Citibank canceled the card and the employee was fired for failing to pay off the GICC on time and misusing government funds.

60

Use of Fellow Soldiers' Government Credit Cards Earns Reprimand

While conducting operations in Kuwait, an Army Major in the Corps Support Group Advance Party needed a number of mission-essential items. He ordered these items with several Government Purchase Cards (GPCs). The only problem, the cards were not his. Before deployment, the Major had managed to collect a list of the numbers and security codes of GPCs held by members of his unit who were not deploying. These cardholders then noticed a rash of unexplained payments from Kuwait. As cardholders are personally responsible for the charges on their cards, several cardholders disputed the charges in accordance with regulations. This led to a long series of unnecessary and frustrating exchanges with the credit card company.

As a result of his actions, the Major received counseling. While there was no evidence that he had used the cards for personal purchases, his use was unauthorized. GPCs can only be used by their authorized cardholder with the consent of an Approving Official. Unauthorized use bypasses the safeguards created to minimize abuse.

Credit Card Abuse and Misuse of Resources Results in Suspension

An IT Specialist with the Defense Information Systems Agency (DISA) was reprimanded for a trio of offenses committed over the span of a year. Investigators found that the specialist used his DISA Government travel card to pay for $2,735.45 worth of food, gas, and rental cars while on personal trips to Indiana to visit his girlfriend. The specialist additionally claimed per diem allowances for two days on which he was technically Absent Without Leave (AWOL). Finally, the specialist used his Government cell phone to make personal phone calls such that unofficial use comprised anywhere from 30-50% of his total usage.

The specialist was suspended for three days, reimbursed the Government $1,384.38 for his cell phone abuse, paid off his Government credit card, and took two days of leave to account for his period AWOL.

Running Up the Government "IMPAC" Card

The Facts: A (former) civilian director of the Pentagon's Graphics and Presentation Division used her Government-issued, Merchant Purchase Authorization Card ("IMPAC") to make 522 fake purchases from a Seattle company created by a fellow schemer solely to carry out the fraud. Payments by the Government for the "purchases" were made to the Seattle firm, but the co-schemer would simply cash the checks and split the "take" with the director. The director was caught and sentenced to three years and one month in prison and was ordered to pay $1.7 million in restitution.

The Law: Don't steal. Theft violates various state and Federal laws.

Senior NCO Abuses Government Credit Card

An investigation concluded that a senior U.S. Marine improperly used his Government credit card by purchasing gas for his personal vehicle, dinners, and concert tickets as well as obtaining cash advances—all unrelated to official travel.

The Marine was counseled by his supervisor and required to reimburse the Government for all unauthorized purchases. He retired soon after the investigation.

DoD Employee Charges Caribbean Vacation to Government Credit Card

A GS-13 Department of Defense employee used her Government credit card to pay for her personal vacation to the Caribbean. The case was referred to the U.S. Attorney, who declined prosecution. The employee was counseled by her supervisor and warned that if any other inappropriate charges were made on her account she would be disciplined. (Yes, she reimbursed the Government.)

Department of Defense Employee Makes $6,000 in Personal Charges

An investigation revealed that a Department of Defense civilian employee had made inappropriate, personal charges in the amount of over $6,000 using his government travel card. The employee was suspended without pay for failing to follow the terms of the credit card use policy.

Public Official Misuses Credit Card

A Department of Energy employee recently pled guilty to a theft of Government property charge. The employee made over $7,000 in personal charges on her Government credit card by hiding the charges among legitimate Government purchases. The employee also falsified invoices and credit card records to further conceal the purchases. The employee was sentenced to two years probation and ordered to pay restitution for the amount of the charges.

Department of Veterans Affairs Employee Misuses Credit Card

A former Department of Veterans Affairs employee recently pled guilty to one count of theft of Government property. The former employee used her Government credit card to purchase expensive items (TVs were a favorite), which she then re-sold or kept for herself. The judge sentenced her to five years' probation and ordered her to pay $170,000 in restitution.

Department of Defense Civilian Employee Misuses Credit Card

A Department of Defense civilian employee recently pled guilty to one count of theft of Government property. The employee entered into an arrangement with two vendors in which they would charge the Government credit card for non-existent goods and services. The vendors would then give cash to the DoD employee. The vendors charged over $12,000 and kicked back $3,000 to the employee. The employee was sentenced to two years of probation with four months home confinement, and was ordered to pay $12,473 in restitution and a $1,000 fine.

U.S. Government IMPAC Credit Card Abuse by Air Force Employees

Three former civilian employees from Barksdale Air Force Base, Louisiana, were convicted of conspiracy to defraud the Government (18 U.S.C. 371) and conversion of U.S. property for personal use (18 U.S.C. 641). The employees used the U.S. Government IMPAC credit cards to purchase personal items, which included extensive home improvement products and car-related materials. One of the employees certified on official documents that purchases on the IMPAC credit card were properly used by members of the reserve unit.

One of the employees was sentenced to a one year and one day prison term, and the other employees were sentenced to six months in a Federal halfway house and were required to make full restitution.

Cardholder Supervisor Convicted for Credit Card Abuse

The supervisor of four IMPAC cardholders was convicted for misusing Government credit cards. The supervisor used the credit card numbers of his four subordinates, none of whom were suspected of any wrongdoing, to make multiple purchases from a local auto parts store and a military surplus store. The supervisor then proceeded to re-sell most of the products at his bar. Some of the items purchased included gas grills, truck parts, and automobile tires. The supervisor convinced the managers of the auto parts store and the military surplus store to alter the credit card invoices to list what would appear to be official military supplies, instead of listing the actual goods purchased. The evidence indicates that the DoD supervisor defrauded the Government to the tune of $200,000.

The employee pled guilty to violating 18 U.S.C. 287, for submitting false and fraudulent claims, and 18 U.S.C. 208, for approving the fraudulent purchases. He was sentenced to ten months in prison.

Accountant Goes to Jail for Misuse of Travel Card

A supervisory accountant at the National Science Foundation (NSF) found herself at the receiving end of criminal charges for government travel card abuse—a situation that should have come as no surprise, given that her responsibilities included managing the NSF's travel card program. Investigators found that on forty-seven separate occasions, the accountant used her travel card to make personal purchases and unauthorized cash withdrawals. When the Investigator General began an audit of the travel card program, the accountant purged her own transactions from the records in an (unsuccessful) attempt to hide her misuse.

The formerly footloose accountant was saddled with a $1,000 fine and sentenced to 20 weekends in jail as a condition of a two-year probation. Her misuse of the travel card not only ended her career at NSF, but barred her from all future federal employment. Government travel cards should only be used for expenses related to official travel.

Employee Faces 10 Years for Theft of Credit Cards

Following up on two stolen Government credit cards, investigators cut short the entrepreneurial career of a utility worker for the Norfolk Naval Station Public Works Center. After stealing the two cards, which were used to gas fleet vehicles, the worker began to offer to fill the tanks of other gas station patrons in exchange for cash valuing half the pump price. The worker's popularity was short-lived, however, as investigators quickly noticed the sudden boom at the pumps. An internal audit conducted by the Navy revealed that the loss to the Government from the two purloined cards totaled $44,866.

The employee faces a maximum sentence of ten years imprisonment and a fine of $250,000.

Friend's Credit Card Use Costs Employee $13,000

An Army recruiter in Christiansburg, Virginia paid the price for gifting a Government credit card to a friend – literally. When the recruiter's office issued the recruiter a Government Fleet credit card, he magnanimously decided to give the card to his friend. His friend subsequently used the now-stolen card for personal expenditures totaling over $13,000, including gasoline, automotive parts, and food. The recruiter's "generosity" was amply rewarded by the District Court judge, who sentenced him to two years of probation and held him liable for the total $13,000 spent by his friend.

The Government Fleet credit card program provides for the maintenance of Government owned and leased vehicles and is only to be used by authorized employees for official purposes.

Federal Employee Stole Credit Card Numbers to Hire Prostitutes

A former Transportation Department employee pled guilty to one count of wire fraud for using counterfeit checks and stolen credit card information to hire prostitutes while conducting official Government business. The Federal employee, who has begun treatment for sexual addiction, accumulated at least $39,000 from over 100 escort services. The employee stole his colleagues' credit card numbers and the receipts of random strangers that he found left on restaurant tables. The employee admitted he often pretended to be the senior vice president of a publicly traded company during his "shopping" trips. A court sentenced the official to serve six months house arrest and three years of probation.

(Source: International Herald Tribune, March 13, 2007)

Endorsements

SES Uses Title to Promote Non-Federal Entity

A Senior Executive Service employee served on the board of directors of a non-Federal entity (NFE). While on the board, he listed his official position and DoD contact information on the NFE's Web site. Prior to this ethical violation, he had failed to request a legal opinion regarding his ties to the NFE. He was counseled and told to remove his title from NFE materials.

Service Officer Sanctions Website by Wearing Uniform

A Service officer allowed her photograph, while wearing her uniform, to appear on the website of a non-federal organization. The website identified her as a Board Member of the organization. The posting created the impression the officer was participating in the management of the NFE in her official capacity, or alternatively, that the Federal Government endorsed the organization (in violation of 5 C.F.R. 2635.702(b). The officer was verbally counseled and the picture on the website was cropped to cover the uniform.

Be Careful from Here Onward

Seven senior military officers, including four Generals, were found to have misused their positions, improperly implying DoD endorsement or support of a Non-Federal Entity while appearing in a promotional video for the Christian Embassy. A Pentagon Chaplain arranged for Christian Embassy employees to obtain Pentagon building passes for filming. The video showed interviews conducted at recognizable Pentagon locations, featuring the senior officers in uniform and displaying their ranks as they discussed their Christian faith. Two SES Government employees who appeared in the video without title and whose comments did not create the appearance of DoD sanction were found to have properly participated in their personal capacity. The military officers, however, violated Paragraph 3-209 of DoD 5500.07-R, Joint Ethics Regulation which prohibits actions by employees suggesting DoD endorsement of Non-Federal Entities, and C.F.R. 2635.702 which prohibits using one's public office for private endorsement.

Financial Disclosure Violations

Valley Fraud

A former official of the Tennessee Valley Authority (TVA) received two years' probation and was ordered to pay a $5,000 fine and perform 150 hours of community service for failing to disclose information on his financial disclosure form. John Symonds pled guilty to violating 18 U.S.C. § 1001 for making a false material statement by failing to disclose information regarding the receipt of money from a source other than his U.S. Government salary on his financial disclosure form.

While working as a manager for TVA from November 2000 through December 2002, Symonds was required to complete an Executive Branch Confidential Financial Disclosure Report, Office of Government Ethics (OGE) Form 450, as well as update his financial disclosure report annually by submitting Optional OGE Form 450-A. Despite owning a company that received over $50,000 in 2002 from another company, Symonds filed an OGE Form 450-A certifying that he had no new reportable assets or sources of income. Symonds and his former spouse used the payments for personal expenses.

Failure to Report Gifts From Abramoff Gets DOI Official Two-Years of Probation

A former Department of the Interior Officer who accepted Washington Redskins tickets, which cost over $2,000, as well as other gifts from lobbyist Jack Abramoff, was sentenced to two years of probation, and to pay a $1,000 fine. Abramoff was seeking official action from the officer when he gave the officer the gifts. The officer failed to disclose these gifts on the required financial disclosure report (Form 450), and after being investigated in connection with the Abramoff scandal, he pled guilty to making a false certificate or writing. Public officials who are required to file a Form 450 must disclose gifts that exceed a minimum value. Bottom line: if public officials keep secrets about the gifts they receive from sources like lobbyists, they will receive a gift from the federal government that they cannot keep secret — probation.

Lawyer Says Financial Disclosures Are a Nuisance, Client Gets Probation

A world-renowned Alzheimer's research scientist for the National Institutes of Health (NIH) was sentenced to serve two years of probation and four-hundred hours of community service after failing to disclose several hundred-thousand dollars in consulting fees he received for services rendered to a prohibited source — a pharmaceutical company doing business with his agency. The scientist violated a federal conflicts of interest statute and federal regulations requiring him to disclose payments from outside sources on his financial disclosure report (OGE Form 450). The purpose of the required financial disclosure is to help employees recognize conflicting financial interests and avoid violating the law. The scientist's lawyer said that it is common for NIH researchers not to file financial disclosures because they consider the disclosures a "bureaucratic nuisance." Maybe so, but this scientist should have known, as most world-renowned medical researchers probably do, that untreated nuisances often become debilitating illnesses. In addition to probation and four-hundred hours of community service, the scientist was also forced to forfeit the consulting fees he had received from the pharmaceutical company, and was deprived of his retirement from the government.

Consultant Fails to File Financial Disclosure Report, Pays Fine Instead

A DoD Consultant failed to file the final public financial disclosure report when the Consultant's appointment expired. The Consultant received several reminders, but chose to ignore them and never filed the report. Unfortunately, the Consultant was unable to ignore the Department of Justice. After substantial negotiations, the filer agreed to pay a $2,000 fine, to pay the $200 late filing fee, and to file the financial disclosure report that should have been filed in the first place. (And don't forget the attorney fees) Bottom line: Failure to file a financial disclosure report was very costly. (DoD Standards of Conduct Office)

HUD Employee Fails to Disclose Ill-Gotten Real Estate on Financial Disclosure, Loses Job

A HUD employee's spouse-like partner submitted the winning bid for a HUD-owned property. Among other violations, the HUD employee failed to notify the agency that someone with whom she was living was submitting a bid for the property. After the property was purchased, the employee's partner transferred the property to the employee for $1. To prevent HUD from learning that the property came to the employee through a straw-man transaction, the employee failed to list the property on her financial disclosure report as was required. The employee was found to have falsified her financial disclosure report and was fired.

Failing to Report Gift Leads to FBI Agent Resignation

A Supervisory Special Agent (SSA) in the Charlotte, North Carolina FBI field office was forced to resign in the wake of revelations that he had failed to disclose gifts from a suspect in an organized gambling and money laundering investigation. The SSA had been acting head of the White Collar Crime Squad, which was handling the investigation; he had also served as the suspect's official handler after the suspect agreed to cooperate with investigators. Due to his duties, the SSA was required to file an OGE Form 450, the Confidential Financial Disclosure Report. The SSA certified that he had received no gifts or travel reimbursements from any one source totaling more than $260.00. However, investigators soon learned that on two separate occasions, the SSA had accompanied the suspect to Las Vegas, where the suspect paid for the SSA's hotel and gambling expenses. The value of the trips was estimated to be in excess of $6,000.

The SSA pled guilty to 18 U.S.C. 1018, making a false writing. He was forced to resign from the FBI and was sentenced to two years' probation and 400 hours of community service.

$11,000 Fine for Failure to File

The Facts: A former Census Bureau official was assessed the maximum fine when he failed to file his financial disclosure report as required by law upon ending his Government employment. Before his retirement, the official had received multiple memos reminding him of his obligation; after he missed the filing deadline, the official received a number of additional certified letters informing him of the availability of extensions and the consequences of failing to file.

The Department of Commerce eventually referred the matter to the Department of Justice, which filed a complaint alleging that the official knowingly and willingly failed to file a financial disclosure report. Finding the official a totally unresponsive party with flagrant violations, a Federal court entered the default judgment and ordered an $11,000 fine, the top civil penalty permitted under the statute. The court emphasized the flagrancy of the violation, citing the employee's choice to ignore the multiple notices and warnings provided to him.

(Source: United States v. Gant, No. 02-2312, 2003 U.S. Dist. LEXIS 10620 (D.D.C. June 17, 2003)

The Law: The Ethics in Government Act (EIGA), 5 U.S.C. app. § 101 et seq. (2003), requires senior officials, who file SF 278s, to file a final financial disclosure report "on or before the thirtieth day" after termination of their senior positions (in addition to annual filing requirements). Anyone who knowingly and willfully fails to provide such a disclosure faces prosecution and fines of up to $10,000 (*see* 5 U.S.C. app. § 101(e)-(f), app. § 104).

D.C. Mayor Financial Disclosure

The failure to report $40,000 he had earned in consulting contracts cost the Mayor of Washington, D.C., $1000 several years ago. The Mayor violated the city's campaign finance code by neglecting to report these earnings on his financial disclosure report.

Under 5 C.F.R. 2634.701, willful failure to file a public financial disclosure report (OGE Form 278) or willful falsification of any information required to be reported may result in administrative actions or $10,000 in civil penalties. In addition, criminal actions may be brought against Federal officials who provide false information on their financial disclosure reports.

Former Government Official Convicted of Filing False Disclosure Report

A former Chief of Staff (CoS) for the Secretary of Agriculture was required to file a Public Financial Disclosure Report (OGE Form 278) under the Ethics in Government Act. While in office, the CoS and his wife received payments totaling approximately $22,025 from two businessmen who were longtime friends and business associates of the CoS – and who coincidentally – received subsidies from the Department of Agriculture (USDA) totaling $63,000 and $284,000, respectively. The CoS was required to, but did not, report these payments on his OGE Form 278. While the USDA Inspector General was conducting an investigation of the CoS with respect to conflict of interest allegations, the CoS made a sworn declaration that he had not received such payments. He also stated that his only income from the time he became Chief of Staff, aside from the sale of a former residence, was his USDA salary.

The former CoS was convicted of violating 18 U.S.C. 1001, for failing to properly disclose the payments received from the two businessmen and for making a false sworn statement to the USDA Inspector General. He was sentenced to 27 months in jail.

Former EEOC Chairman Failed to File Financial Disclosure Report

The former chairman of the Equal Employment Opportunity Commission settled a lawsuit brought by the Department of Justice for $4,000. The lawsuit alleged that the chairman did not file a required financial disclosure report for two years that he was in Government service. In the previous year, the chairman filed the yearly financial disclosure report required of all senior executive branch employees (SF 278). For the subsequent two years, however, he submitted a photocopy of the first year's report. The Chairman acknowledged that the photocopied report did not reflect changes in his income. He further maintained that the inaccuracy was inadvertent and the result of a mistake made in good faith. The Director of the Office of Government Ethics noted that the chairman did not respond to four requests to file the required report over the course of two years.

Former FDA Commissioner Convicted for False Financial Disclosures and Conflict of Interest

The U.S. District Court for the District of Columbia sentenced a former Commissioner of the Food and Drug Administration (FDA) to serve three years of probation, along with 50 hours of community service, and to pay fines totaling $89,377.36. The former Commissioner pled guilty to two misdemeanor charges involving false financial disclosures and a violation of the conflict of interest statute, 18 U.S.C. 208, which prohibits a Government employee from participating in any activities in which he, his spouse, or minor child has a financial interest.

Between 2002 and 2006, the former Commissioner held several senior positions which required him to certify and file on six occasions a financial disclosure report that included all of his investments valued at more than $1,000. Although the Commissioner declared he and his wife had sold the stock they owned in numerous "significantly regulated organizations," the couple failed to disclose that they actually retained stock in several of the companies. The conflict of interest violation occurred when the Commissioner was acting as the Chairman of the FDA's Obesity Working Group. Investigators discovered two of the companies in which the Commissioner and his wife held stock had a direct financial interest in the group's conclusions. Although there was no evidence that the Commissioner's financial interests altered the group's conclusions, the Court concluded that his participation in the deliberations affected the integrity of group's findings.

(Source: Federal Ethics Report, March 2007)

Fraud (Violations Not Covered Elsewhere)

It does not "Pay" to Play with Fake Poker Chips

The former deputy head of U.S. Strategic Command has learned that it doesn't pay to play with fake poker chips. The former deputy was fired upon revelations that he counterfeited poker chips to use in support of his gambling habit. Investigators substantiated the claims against the flag officer upon discovering his DNA underneath the adhesive tape that was used to alter three $1 chips into $500 chips. Records show the deputy's gambling habit had him spending an average of 15 hours per week—1,096 hours in total—at a casino in Iowa prior to being discovered playing with the counterfeit chips. His misconduct resulted in two convictions for conduct unbecoming an officer for using the altered gambling chips and lying to investigators. In addition to being relieved of his duties at U.S. Strategic Command, the deputy was reduced in rank from three-star to two-star admiral and was transitioned to the retired list at the lower grade.

(Source: Navy Times; published 22 Nov 2014 and Official U.S. Navy Biography)

Posing as Mother?

In August of 2013, the son of a deceased mother was sentenced to 14 months in prison after pleading guilty to stealing about $350,000 by cashing social security and federal annuity checks meant for his long-dead mother. He had negotiated and converted these checks from March 1999 through June 2012.

Mailman Doesn't Deliver the Mail?

A Postal Service employee has learned that it doesn't pay to get lazy on the job. According to the former employee, being "lazy" was the root cause of his failure to deliver over 1,000 pieces of mail during a year-long period, all of which was found in bins on his front porch. Included amongst the largely junk mail pieces were 27 voter ballots as well as over 200 first-class and standard mailings. For his laziness, the employee has pled guilty to misdemeanor mail obstruction. This redefining of "snail mail" has landed him a one-year probation sentence and a $500 fine.

(Source: The Associated Press; published 23 Jan 2015)

A Decade of War Makes For a Decade of Fraud

After over a decade of war in both Iraq and Afghanistan, attorneys at the Department of Justice (DOJ) continue to work at identifying and prosecuting wide spread criminal business dealings related to those conflicts. The conduct has cost American taxpayers anywhere from $31 billion to $60 billion according to The Commission on Wartime Contracting in Iraq and Afghanistan (the Commission). It spans from low-level fraud where individuals bill for services not provided to multi-million dollar bribery cases of industry trying to entice the awarding of contracts. Per one national security academic at George Washington University, the U.S. military was not equipped to provide appropriate oversight and lacked accountability processes. The Department of Justice (DOJ) is pursuing accountability, however, as over 230 criminal cases were brought between 2005 and 2014 according to the Commission. One of the most recent cases stemmed from a former officer taking advantage of the Army's G-RAP program that provided bonus pay to active duty members who referred new recruits to join the military. This program, now discontinued, was riddled with cases where service members claimed bonuses for referrals that were never made. The officer, who was found to have claimed $118,000 as a result of 119 false referrals, has been sentenced to no less than three years in prison according to the DOJ. *(Source: AP News; 17 Nov 2014)*

Your Posters are My Posters

An army officer was convicted both for making false statements, including false statements in his confidential financial disclosure report (failure to report an outside position and the income from that position), and for stealing government property. The employee put in an order at the department print shop, certifying that a series of posters were for official business. The posters were actually for the employee's side business. Additionally, the employee purchased a conference table, for which his own business got a $400 credit toward a conference table of its own. The employee was sentenced to 2 years of probation, 6 months house arrest, a fine of $25,000, and was ordered to pay $1,600 in restitution.

Service-member Pockets BAH Money

For two years after his divorce, an active duty service-member continued to list his ex-wife on his Basic Allowance for Housing paperwork, allowing him to pocket extra funds, including a family separation allowance. While the overpayment continued for two years, the service-member continued to keep the money. Once the command caught on, he was court martialed, sentenced to six months confinement, fined, and reduced in rank.

Veterinarian Technicians Pocket Thousands

An E-6 and E-4, both veterinarian technicians for a service, received Basic Allowance for Housing to which they were not entitled. They lived in base housing while receiving overpayments. They took no action to report the mistake. Overall, the Government lost more than $26,000. Both service-members were reduced in rank and ordered to repay all funds.

"I thought they were mine."

A government contractor stole eight 40-foot Container Express (CONEX) shipping/storage units valued at $56,000 from a Service base in the United States. Investigators found two stolen government license plates on the contractor's personal vehicles, used to access the base. The contractor claimed he thought the CONEX units were abandoned. He was charged with grand larceny and debarred from doing business with the government.

"I do" ... Though I Don't Even Know You

Six Service members stationed in the United States were arrested and charged with defrauding the government for their part in a scheme to marry Russian women in exchange for drawing military benefits. The brother of one of the service-members set up the introduction to the Russian women while living in New York. The service-members then filed false basic allowance for housing (BAH) and family separation allowance (FSA) claims for their absent wives that defrauded the government of over $234,000. The investigation revealed most of the men never actually lived with their so-called wives. The service-members were court-martialed, reduced in rank, and ordered to pay restitution equaling the amount of money each received fraudulently. The women, who obtained visas enabling them to stay in the States as a result of the false marriages, were deported.

Side Business Ends Service Supply Chief's Career

A Service Chief storekeeper for a submarine in the United States was found guilty of using ship's funds to buy merchandise to later sell for his personal gain. The Chief made off with over $90,000 of unauthorized items including watches, computers, PDAs, TVs, chairs, and cameras, which he stored in his personal room until selling. He was court-martialed and sentenced to two years in prison, reduced down to an E-1, separated under a bad conduct discharge, and ordered to pay $25,000 in fines. His immediate supervisor, a junior Service officer, was administratively separated from the Service. $75,000 worth of merchandise was never recovered.

New York State of Mind

A Service sergeant was court-martialed for fraud and larceny of government funds, for knowingly submitting false basic allowance for housing (BAH) claims for three years while stationed overseas. The sergeant claimed his wife and kids were living in New York City, the highest BAH city in the system, while they were actually living in Puerto Rico. The sergeant received over $50,000 he was not entitled to under the false claims. He was sentenced to twelve years in prison, reduced to E-1, and dishonorably discharged.

Married or Not?

A soldier got married and provided his marriage certificate to the Service, but shortly after the marriage his wife returned to her home in another state. Nine months later the marriage was annulled. The soldier did not report that he was no longer married, and continued to collect a housing allowance for himself and his now former wife. He also listed her on travel reimbursements and received additional per diem for trips where she did not accompany him. In total, the soldier was paid approximately $45,000 in funds that he was not eligible to receive.

At some point, the soldier appeared to sense that he was going to be caught because he tried to throw off the investigation by filing for divorce even though the marriage had been annulled much earlier. He then informed investigators that he was not aware that the marriage had been annulled prior to his divorce filing. The ruse was not particularly effective because court records showed the soldier was physically present at the annulment hearing. His case was referred for court martial.

Imaginary Ball and Chain Drags Staff Sergeants Down

An Army Staff Sergeant stationed at Ft. Bragg, North Carolina continued to receive Basic Allowance for Housing (BAH) at the married rate even after he was divorced from his wife. He knowingly and willfully failed to submit documentation to reflect this change, thus receiving more money than he was entitled to and therefore committing fraud and larceny. The Staff Sergeant was charged with larceny under the Uniform Code of Military Justice and found guilty by General Court Martial. He was sentenced to five months in confinement, forfeiture of $5,000 and a reduction in grade from Staff Sergeant (E-6) to Private First Class (E-3). In a similar case, a Staff Sergeant at U.S. Army CENTCOM was caught illegally receiving BAH at the higher married rate when he was actually single. The soldier submitted a false marriage license, ultimately receiving $15,100 in Basic Allowance for Housing and Family Separation Allowance to which he was not entitled. His "wife" also fraudulently received $13,200 in Tricare healthcare benefits. The relationship must have gone sour though, because she ended up turning him in to military investigators. After such a betrayal, one can only assume he will now be filing for a fake divorce.

All-Expenses Paid Bachelor Pad with Maid Service Included?

A Lieutenant Commander working as the Naval Station Great Lakes Bachelor Housing Officer misused Government resources when he lived in the quarters without cost and received free housekeeping and amenities. He was charged on three counts under the Uniform Code of Military Justice (Articles 81, 92, and 134) and issued a Letter of Reprimand as a form of Non-Judicial Punishment. A civilian Government official who was aware of the Lieutenant Commander's illegal conduct, but failed to report it was also issued a Letter of Reprimand for violating the Basic Obligation of Public Service requiring that he disclose any known fraud, waste, abuse, and corruption (C.F.R. 2635.101(b)(11)).

Handling Service Members' Injury Claims Wounds Government Financially

A Navy civilian Medicare claims examiner was employed to represent Government interests in the settlement of Medical Care Recovery Act (MCRA) claims. Her job entailed regularly negotiating with insurance companies and injured military personnel in order to recover Government expenditures on medical care for service members and their dependents who were injured due to the acts of uninsured third parties. Although the Navy has authority to waive its claims on behalf of injured service members against insurance companies, the examiner orchestrated a scheme in which she used her position and authority to waive claims and to fraudulently obtain money for herself that was owed to the Government. In one case, the examiner handled the claim for a Petty Officer who had been injured in a motorcycle accident. She told the service member that she could increase the amount of his settlement if he agreed to split the amount with her. When he agreed, the examiner notified the insurance company that the Navy was waiving its MRCA claim. When the company sent the Petty Officer a $6,000 check, he sent her $3,000 cash just as she had directed. It turned out that the Petty Officer had been working with law enforcement authorities all along.

The U.S. Attorney prosecuted the examiner and obtained a conviction for one count of Mail Fraud. She was sentenced to two months in prison, two years of probation, a $100 special assessment, and was debarred by the Navy for three years.

Invoices Submitted on Behalf of MakeBelieveCompany, Inc.

A civilian employee and Government purchase card holder working at the Naval Surface Warfare Center (NSWC) in Maryland conspired with an outside vendor to create fraudulent invoices in the name of fictitious companies such as Greenway Supply, Government Supply, and Aerospace Technologies. The invoices fraudulently showed that these imaginary companies had provided goods and services to NSWC when in fact no products or services were ever provided. The Government employee used his purchase card to pay for hundreds of such invoices, all in amounts of less than $2,500 so as to avoid attracting too much scrutiny. When NSWC took away the employee's purchase card, the vendor continued to submit the false invoices in cooperation with a second employee. Ultimately, the vendor made between $200,000 and $400,000 in profit from the conspiracy. All three people involved were guilty of making false and fraudulent statements to the Government and embezzling money belonging to NSWC. The vendor pled guilty to one count of conspiracy to defraud the Government, 18 U.S.C. §371. The Navy debarred the vendor and both employees for three years.

Marine Corp Says Goodbye to Officers who Schemed with Thai Vendors

Three U.S. Marine Corps Forces Pacific, Joint U.S. Military Group, Thailand (JUSMAGTHAI) officers were caught receiving bribes and kickbacks from a Thai vendor. A Naval Criminal Investigative Service investigation revealed that a Marine Corps Major, either directly or through his wife, accepted approximately $100,000 in gifts from a Thai vendor, to include a truck and a loan for a house. The Major continued to engage in business with the vendor and awarded him contracts, but did not disclose his personal financial conflict of interest to his agency designee as mandated by 18 U.S.C. §208. He also passed inside information to the vendor, allowing her to increase her bid while still ensuring she was the lowest bidder and therefore increasing her profit margin. He was also charged with maintaining a sexual relationship with a woman who was not his wife, which is illegal under the Uniform Code of Military Justice. Another Marine Corps Major received gifts, including free hotel rooms, from a prohibited source in violation of 10 U.S.C. section 892 and section 933. A third Marine Corps

Major also worked with the vendor to defraud the Government. The Major, taking advantage of his position as the first person in the logistics chain to come into contact with goods and services provided by contractors, signed receipts for delivery of purchase orders even though the vendor had only delivered incomplete shipments. The Government was nonetheless billed the cost of full shipment, while the conspiring parties split the profits from these "ghost shipments." The Major signed orders for at least five ghost shipments and received $2,324 in bribes for his participation. All three Majors were debarred from Government contracting by the Navy Acquisition Integrity Office. Furthermore, they were all charged under the Uniform Code of Military Justice. The first Major was dismissed from active duty, sentenced to four years in confinement and a $25,000 fine. The second Major received a Punitive Letter of Reprimand and was subjected to a $3,060 forfeiture of pay. The third Major was discharged and sent to spend six months in the brig.

Overpricing by Contractor Results in $44,000 Refund

An Army technician ordering a Seal Replacement Parts Kit from a defense contractor noted that the price of the kit seemed unusually high based on the price of each individual component, and contacted investigators. Investigators examined the price of the components and the cost the company incurred to assemble each kit, and discovered that the contractor was marking up each kit by approximately $500. Investigators further discovered that the Government had purchased a large number of the kits at the inflated price.

As a result of the observant technician's number-crunching, the defense contractor agreed to a voluntary refund of $44,000.

Favoritism Results in Senior Official's Resignation

A senior official at the National Defense University left his post after his relationship with a subordinate came to light. Employees told investigators that they had witnessed inappropriate physical contact between the official and a component program director. The official allegedly favored the program director by approving leave requests during critical periods, affording her more authority than her position entitled her, giving her leniency regarding her work schedule, and consistently relying on her opinion above others. The official was also accused of creating a hostile work environment by repeatedly demeaning employees.

The program director was separately charged with misusing Government property by taking excessive leave and misreporting time and attendance.

The official resigned his post, and the program director was detailed to a different component and received counseling.

Contractor Fraud Results in Investigation

Contractors who were awarded a $564 million contract to construct the Olmsted Dam on the Ohio River found themselves high and dry after the discovery of fraudulent reimbursement charges billed to the Government. The contractors had purchased a number of vehicles to be used on the job, and properly billed the purchase cost to the Government. However, investigators discovered that the contractors allowed eight senior-level employees to drive their vehicles home at night as part of an "incentives" program. These contractors were further involved in three accidents with the vehicles, the cost of which was submitted for reimbursement to the Government.

To Defraud or Not To Defraud? That's an Easy Question!

The Facts: An Internal Revenue Service (IRS) officer conspired with two private tax preparers to develop a scheme to defraud the United States Government. The tax preparers told persons owing money to the Government that they could negotiate a lesser debt if they would go ahead and pay off what was owed. The IRS officer would then enter false information into the relevant files showing that the individuals in question had insufficient assets to cover their debts. This convinced the IRS to halt collection efforts. Strangely (or not), the money paid to the tax preparers never made it to the IRS. The tax preparers were sentenced along with the IRS officer, who, for tinkering with the debts of others, ended up with quite a "debt" of her own: She was sentenced to 3 years and one month in prison, to be followed by 3 years of probation, and ordered to pay in restitution $322,135.

The Law: 18 U.S.C. § 371 (2003) authorizes fines and imprisonment for up to five years for anyone conspiring with one or more other persons to defraud the United States, if any one of the conspirators takes any action to carry out the fraud. In this case, all three persons appear to have taken such an act. The IRS officer was also charged under 26 U.S.C. § 7214 (2003) of the Internal Revenue Code, which requires that any IRS officer who conspires to defraud the

Government be discharged from their office and, if convicted, pay up to $10,000 in fines, serve up to five years in prison, or both.

Conflicts of Interest and Lies Garner Federal Convictions
For Alderwoman and Daughters

A Milwaukee alderwoman and her two daughters found themselves as defendants in federal court for funneling city funds to a non-profit organization they had created. The alderwoman, before her election, founded a non-profit organization eligible to carry out neighborhood social grants; it was largely funded by Housing and Urban Development (HUD) grants awarded to the City of Milwaukee. These grants were given to the city upon the condition that each grant recipient complies with HUD regulations. Among these regulations was a conflict-of-interest provision preventing any elected official that participated in the apportionment of the HUD grants from obtaining a financial benefit "either for themselves or those with whom they have business – or immediate family ties."

Upon the alderwoman's election, she turned the executive directorship of the non-profit organization over to her two daughters, who both drew a salary from the organization. Both daughters had different last names from each other as well as the alderwoman, and the relationship between the three was unknown by the City and HUD. After taking office, the alderwoman secured membership on the Community Development Policy Committee, the committee that apportioned HUD grants. She was informed by the City Attorney of the HUD conflict-of-interest rules, and wrote a memo assuring the City that her husband and (singular) daughter only worked for the non-profit on a volunteer basis. This deception persisted the following year, when the City began to suspect a scam; the alderwoman wrote another letter to the city attorney admitting that her (singular) daughter had been an employee of the non-profit, but assuring that she had since left her position (which was untrue). However, by this point, the City was aware of the alderwoman's deception, and she was charged with various violations of federal law.

During the time period the alderwoman was in office, the non-profit accepted a number of lucrative HUD grants from the city. Each contract included a recitation of the HUD conflict-of-interest provisions, and was signed by both daughters in their capacity as executive officers. When queried by the City regarding the familial relation of the two daughters to the alderwoman, the daughters chose not to respond. This duplicity earned both daughters charges in federal court alongside their mother.

The alderwoman and one of her daughters pled guilty to various violations of federal law. The second daughter chose to go to trial, and was convicted and sentenced to two years' probation and a $1000 fine for violating her contractual duty to disclose her familial relationship with the alderwoman.

(Source: 2006 U.S. App. LEXIS 10878)

Employee Gets Ten Years for Authorizing Fraudulent Retirement Benefits

A retirement benefits specialist at the U.S. Office of Personnel Management (OPM) developed an embezzlement scheme that eventually involved 15 cohorts and resulted in the theft of $3.7 million from the Civil Services Retirement Trust Fund. The specialist's duties included authorizing monthly benefits payments as well as one-time payments intended to retroactively adjust Federal benefits. Instead of authorizing payments for the proper recipients, the employee began to authorize payments to fellow employees. The scheme allowed at least 25 people to obtain illegal one-time payments from the Retirement Trust Fund, after which they paid kickbacks to the OPM employees.

The specialist was sentenced to 10 years in prison for her role as the ringleader of the operation. Her coconspirators received lesser terms.

Boyfriends Can Be Very Expensive For Employees Who Steal Funds

A U.S. Forest Service employee faced a maximum of 13 years in prison for stealing over $642,000 and committing tax fraud. The employee paid restitution of the entire $642,000 prior to sentencing.

The employee admitted that during her job of overseeing payments with Federal charge cards and Government checks, she wrote Government checks to her boyfriend, who occasionally contracted with the Forest Service. Disguised as firefighting payments, the checks were deposited in the couple's joint bank account and used to pay for expenses and gambling.

It appears this relationship came at a very high price.

(Source: OregonLive.com)

Contractors and Federal Personnel Working Together, Defraud Government and Go to Jail

An investigation by several Government agencies in support of the Justice Department's National Procurement Fraud Task Force revealed a complex scheme to defraud the Coalition Provisional Authority – South Central Region (CPA-SC) in al-Hillah, Iraq. The perpetrators, a former Department of Defense (DoD) employee, several former soldiers and numerous public officials, including two high-ranking U.S. Army officers, conspired in a fraud and money-laundering plan involving contracts in the reconstruction of Iraq.

The Task Force discovered the co-conspirators connived to rig bids on contracts so that CPA-SC awarded them all to the same contractor. In addition, the conspirators stole over $2 million in currency that CPA-SC had slated for reconstruction. As a reward for their efforts, the contractor provided the officials with a variety of gifts, including over $1 million in cash, sports cars, jewelry, computers, liquor, and offers of future employment.

The Task Force charged a former Lieutenant Colonel, two active Lieutenant Colonels, a Colonel and two civilians in a 25-count indictment. The court sentenced the civilian DoD employee to serve 12 months in prison, while the former Lieutenant Colonel earned 21 months in prison for his role. Another former soldier received nine years in prison and a forfeiture of $3.6 million for charges of conspiracy, bribery, and money laundering, as well as weapons possession charges.

The contractor at the center of the conspiracy pled guilty to related charges, and received a 46 month prison sentence. In addition, the court ordered him to forfeit $3.6 million.

(Department of Justice 07-449, June 25, 2007, www.usdoj.gov)

Official Steals Himself Jail Time

A former Intelligence Contingency Funds (ICF) officer for the Department of Defense stole over $100,000 from his former employer. The ICF official pled guilty to one count of theft and embezzlement of Government property, admitting that over a period of three years he had used his official position to withdraw cash from a Government bank account. By falsifying DoD accounting vouchers and forms, the official increased his own bank account with DoD funds while he performed his official budgeting, disbursing, and accounting duties for ICF.

The U.S. District Judge sentenced the official to serve 12 months in prison, pay $106,500 in restitution, and serve three years of supervised release.

(Source: Department of Justice 07-416, June 8, 2007)

Gambling and Other Contest Violations

Federal Employee Rides into Trouble

A local motorcycle dealer sponsored a "motorcycle poker" event across public lands. The off-road bikes followed a pre-set route, stopping along the way to pick up playing cards. The one with the best poker hand at the end won a new motorcycle. The winner? The on-duty Government employee who was to follow the contestants, making sure that nobody had fallen off his bike or gotten lost. He didn't get to keep the bike because he won the prize while carrying out his official duty. While section 2635.203(b)(5) of the Standards of Ethical Conduct for Executive Branch Employees allows Federal employees to keep prizes in contests that are open to the public and not related to the employee's official duties, in this case, the employee won while performing official duties.

Fantasy Football IS Gambling

Gambling allegations were made against a Department of Defense employee who was operating a "fantasy football league" in his workplace. The participants each paid $20 to participate. The funds were used for a luncheon at the end of the season and trophies were purchased for the winners.

Although upon the surface the "fantasy football league" does not appear to be gambling per se, the General Counsel ruled that the activities constituted gambling in the workplace in violation of paragraph 2-302 of DoD 5500.07-R, Joint Ethics Regulation.

NOTE: This case occurred prior to the passage of 31 U.S.C. 5362.

Fantasy Football IS Gambling II

Allegations were made regarding Air National Guard members running a "fantasy football" league on Government computers. Each member of the league contributed $10 to play, with the winner buying all of the other participants' pizza at the end of the season. It was determined that the winner actually expended more on the pizza than the amount of the winnings. It was also determined that activities associated with the game were conducted on break and lunch times.

Section 2-302 of DoD 5500.07-R, Joint Ethics Regulation, prohibits gambling by DoD personnel while on duty or while on Federal property. In addition, it was a misuse of Government resources to carry out such an activity on Government computers. The guardsmen involved were counseled by their commanding officer.

Gambling Ring Garners Federal Charges

Tipped off by a coworker, investigators discovered that a painter at the Department of the Interior was running a full-fledged gambling operation on Government premises. While on official duty, the painter received betting slips from other employees and made payoffs. The painter's subsequent threatening phone call to the tipster earned him a further charge of conduct unbecoming a Federal employee.

41 C.F.R. § 102-74.395 forbids all persons entering in or on Federal property from participating in games for money or other personal property, operating gambling devices, conducting a lottery or pool, or selling or purchasing numbers tickets.

Gift Violations

Apparently VA Stands For "Valuable Appetite"

The Merit Systems Protection Board (MSPB) has upheld the Department of Veterans Affairs' (VA) firing of one of its regional healthcare system directors. The firing, coming in the wake of one of the biggest VA scandals to date, was upheld based on the director's acceptance of a number of "inappropriate gifts" including a trip to Disneyland for her family costing $11,000 and $729 for Beyoncé concert tickets. These gifts were offered by a consultant in the Phoenix area whose job is to land government contracts. Veterans and watchdog groups liken the VA and MSPB decisions to Al Capone's conviction based on tax evasion and not his gangster misgivings given the severity of other accusations levied against her. The most enraging of these accusations was that she knew or should have known of subordinates lying about healthcare wait times for veterans in her Phoenix region—many of who have severe illness ranging from post-traumatic-stress disorder to cancer. Notwithstanding the scathing, yet unsubstantiated, accusations of misrepresenting wait times, having received nearly $12,000 in kick-backs from an industry consultant was more than enough to secure the director's forced retirement.

(Source: The Washington Post; published 26 Dec 2014)

Field Activity Employee Solicitation

An employee recently received a letter of warning for soliciting donations while on duty on a military installation. As a general rule, employees are barred from soliciting gifts while on duty. This employee, however, whether ignorant, defiant, or indifferent to the rules, spent a week asking individuals visiting the base if they would be willing to donate items for a school event. In doing so, the employee, according to witness testimony, would actually accompany willing individuals around and point out items to be bought and donated. Upon purchase, the employee would spend additional time preparing and wrapping the gifts. The letter of warning included a discussion of his violations such as gift solicitations, misuse of official position, and misuse of government time.

(Source: Department of Defense, Office of the Inspector General; 2015)

A Gold-Plated Retirement

A former General commanding U.S. forces in South Korea improperly accepted over $5,000 in gifts and cash, including gold-plated pens, from a South Korean benefactor. The General claimed that the gifts were accepted because the South Korean was a longtime and personal friend, despite the fact that the South Korean did not speak English and they were forced to communicate through hand signals and gestures. The General repaid the South Korean in full and was allowed to retire at a lower grade.

Sampling of Gift Not Sufficient

A Lieutenant Colonel committed dereliction of duty when, in violation of the JER, he received a bottle of Ballantines 30 year-old Scotch valued at $400 and failed to report it and properly dispose of it. In lieu of a court martial, the colonel resigned from the military service for the good of the service under other than honorable conditions.

Like a Private Helicopter Ride to Work? How About a Model Ship?

The Facts: According to sworn testimony and documentation acquired by the office of a military service Inspector General, a senior military officer accepted gifts from the owner of a corporation that serviced and provided landing facilities for military aircraft. The gifts to the officer included a helicopter ride to work, a shirt with the corporation's logo, a miniature model airplane, meals at a Christmas party, and a leather jacket. The officer allegedly returned the jacket but did nothing to compensate for receipt of the other gifts, the value of which exceeded (and probably well exceeded) $100. This conduct occurred as one of a series of alleged offenses that resulted in the officer being relieved of command, issued a punitive letter of reprimand, and ordered to forfeit $1000.

The Law: 5 C.F.R. § 2635.101(b)(14) (2003) requires all Federal employees to avoid any actions that a reasonable person, who knew the relevant facts, could take to be a violation of the law—including the prohibition on providing "preferential treatment to any private organization or individual," mentioned at § 2635.101(b)(8). In this case, the value of the gifts the officer accepted could make it appear that he might influence Government contracting in favor of the corporation. To be sure, he enjoyed some neat gifts—for a time. However: "Public service is a public trust," and it requires that Federal employees place loyalty to "the laws and ethical principles above private gain" (§ 2635.101(b)(1)).

Even more directly on point, 5 C.F.R. §§ 2635.202(a) and 2635.203(d) apply the general principles mentioned above by prohibiting Federal employees from (among other things) soliciting gifts or accepting gifts—whether solicited or not—from any person who "[d]oes business or seeks to do business with the employee's agency."

There are some exceptions to these rules. 5 C.F.R. § 2635.204, for example, allows the acceptance of "unsolicited gifts having an aggregate market value of $20 or less per source per occasion," provided that the value of gifts accepted under the "$20 rule" from a single source do not amount to more than $50 in a given *calendar year*. In the case above, the officer's gifts exceeded (probably well exceeded) this limit.

If you have received a gift or gifts and anticipate that it has put you in jeopardy of violating these, or any other, regulations, 5 C.F.R. § 2635.205 tells you what you must do — and that does not include covering it over (which might make things worse). First, if the gift is an item and not an activity like a helicopter ride, you may return it to the giver or pay the giver the fair market value (see subsection (a)(1)). If that is not practical, you may — "at the discretion of the employee's supervisor or an agency ethics official" —donate the item to an appropriate charity, share the item with your office, or destroy the item (see sub-section (a)(2)). For an activity or event, you obviously can't return the gift, but you can and must pay back the giver the market value of the gift; simply giving back something similar will *not* suffice (see sub-section (a)(3)). If an employee "on his own initiative, promptly complies with the requirements of this section" (that is, § 2635.205), and the gift was not solicited by the employee, then he or she will not be considered to have improperly received that gift.

"Great dinner, thanks for the tip."

Just prior to a major contract award, a Bureau Director went out to dinner with one of the potential competitors at a swanky Washington restaurant. The wine alone cost over $100 per bottle. Too bad the Director didn't realize that a *Washington Post* reporter was at the next table. The story received front-page coverage in the next day's *Post*. By that afternoon, the Director announced that he had accepted a job in private industry — a job he couldn't refuse (with his father-in-law).

The Standards of Ethical Conduct for Employees of the Executive Branch (5 C.F.R. Part 2635) generally prohibit Federal personnel from accepting gifts (including meals) from persons who do business or seek to do business with the employee's agency.

One Party Too Many

The Big Boss was retiring and his second-in-command called the secretary to ask her to set up a retirement party. He directed her to send a memo to the staff advising them of what they were expected to contribute. She was assigned paper plates, napkins, plastic utensils, and a paper tablecloth. Everyone, including the secretary, was expected to contribute $25 for food and gifts. To the surprise of no one, the second-in-command was selected as the new Big Boss. *His* new branch chief called the secretary to have her set up a "promotion" party. The branch chief's memo to the staff advised them of what they were expected to contribute. For the secretary, it was once again paper plates, napkins, plastic utensils and paper tablecloth. Everyone, including the secretary, was again expected to contribute $25 for food and gifts. To no one's surprise, the branch chief was selected as the new second-in-command. *Her* senior analyst called the secretary and asked her to set up a "promotion" party . . . The secretary contacted the Ethics Office instead, where disciplinary action was initiated.

Subpart C of the Standards of Ethical Conduct for Employees of the Executive Branch (5 C.F.R. 2635) establishes the rules for gifts between employees. In general an employee may not give a gift or make a donation to a gift to a superior. Furthermore, employees may not generally accept gifts from other employees who receive less pay. There are certain exceptions, of course.

Gift from a Prohibited Source

As a gesture of thanks, a retailer gave an Army soldier a briefcase after the soldier, using his Government credit card, had purchased office supplies from the retailer. The soldier accepted the briefcase in violation of the Standards of Ethical Conduct for Employees of the Executive Branch (5 C.F.R. Part 2635), which generally ban acceptance of gifts by Federal personnel from persons who do business or seek to do business with the employee's agency. After an investigation, the soldier returned the briefcase and was counseled.

Gift from Subordinate Results in Removal

A Supervisory Contract Specialist at Andrews Air Force Base was terminated after it was discovered that she had accepted a total of $2820 from a subordinate (a subordinate that the specialist had, in fact, personally hired) on two occasions.

Despite the specialist's claims that she did not know that accepting the gifts was wrong, an Administrative Judge affirmed the termination of a 20-year federal career.

5 C.F.R. Part 2635, the "Standards of Ethical Conduct for Employees of the Executive Branch," forbids employees from accepting gifts from lesser-paid employees unless

(1) the employees are not in a subordinate-superior relationship, *and* (2) there is a personal relationship between the two employees that would justify the gift.

Employee Cited for Improperly Accepting Pharmaceutical Samples

The Department of Veterans Affairs (VA) conducted an investigation after it found that an employee at the VA Medical Center at Chillicothe, Ohio, had misused his position and improperly solicited and accepted pharmaceutical drug samples. Upon questioning, the employee acknowledged accepting five different medications from representatives of four pharmaceutical companies, gifts totaling approximately $600. The pharmaceutical representative required a physician to sign for the samples. While a physician did indeed sign off, he testified that he only did so due to pressure from the employee. The investigation uncovered agency-wide confusion regarding the acceptance of drug samples.

Federal gift rules prohibit an employee from accepting or soliciting a gift from a person doing business with the employee's agency. An employee may accept unsolicited gifts having a market value of $20 or less per occasion, provided that the aggregate market value of individual gifts from any one person does not exceed $50 in a calendar year. There is no exception, however, that allows for the acceptance of solicited gifts. In response to the agency-wide problem identified in the investigation, VA officials issued a statement explaining the application of the Federal gift rules to the acceptance of pharmaceutical samples, and developed a fact sheet for agency employees with specific guidance.

Involvement in Claims Against the Government or in Matters Affecting the Government (18 U.S.C. § 205-Type Violations)

Don't Play Attorney Against Your Federal Employer!

The Facts: In the "off-time" from her work with the Social Security Administration, a senior attorney opened her own legal practice and represented clients with claims against that very same Administration. For her double-duty, she was sued by a U.S. Attorney and ended up agreeing to a settlement that required her to pay the United States $113,000 for this and other violations—not a typical attorney's fee!

(Source: Office of Government Ethics memorandum, Oct. 2002)

The Law: 18 U.S.C. § 205 (2003) forbids any current Federal employee from acting as an attorney in prosecuting a claim against the United States—where this is not performed as part of his or her official duties for the Federal Government. For any such violation, the law authorizes fines and possible imprisonment—of not more than one year, unless the conduct is "willful," in which case it can be for up to 5 years (*see* 18 U.S.C. § 216(a)).

Department of Justice Attorney Sentenced for Two Felony Counts

A high-ranking attorney for the Department of Justice was convicted of representing a private party before a Federal Agency in a matter in which the U.S. was a party in interest, in violation of 18 U.S.C. 205. He was also convicted of theft of Government property, in violation of 18 U.S.C. 641. The attorney represented Native Americans before the Department of the Interior in private litigation, and submitted false travel vouchers for Government reimbursement while he served as an employee of the Department of Justice.

The attorney pleaded guilty and was sentenced to four months of home detention and one year of probation. The plea agreement also stipulated that the attorney pay restitution to Department of Justice in the amount of $5,000, pay a $5,000 fine, and pay approximately $2,500 in probation costs. Section 205 prohibits Federal personnel from representing anyone before a Federal Agency or court in connection with a particular matter in which the United States has a direct and substantial interest.

Air Force Civilian Employee Improperly Represents Fellow Employees Before U.S. Government

A civilian employee of the Oklahoma City, Air Logistics Center (OC-ALC), who was also the former OC-ALC shop steward, was charged with violating 18 U.S.C. 205. The employee, who was not an attorney, owned a private company called Associated Labor Consultants. This company provided legal services to other OC-ALC civilian employees by filing legal briefs on behalf of the civilian employees and by representing them before various board hearings against the United States. The employee collected approximately $1,050 in fees from OC-ALC civilian employees for his services, and had billed out but had not collected an additional $1,853.

The Air Force employee was charged with a civil violation of 18 U.S.C. 205. The case was dismissed without prejudice. On February 2, 1998, the parties entered into a stipulated agreement in which the accused agreed to pay the United States $3,000 and to refrain from advising, counseling, or representing persons with claims against the United States.

FAA Employee Improperly Represents Co-worker Before Department of Justice

An engineer employed by the Federal Aviation Administration (FAA) at the Mike Moroney Aeronautical Center in Oklahoma City was charged with violating 18 U.S.C. 205 (among other charges). While employed by the FAA, the engineer attended and graduated from night law school. The new attorney continued his employment as an engineer but prepared wills, powers of attorney, and other legal documents on his own time. Without permission from the FAA, he agreed to represent a fellow FAA employee who was the target of a criminal investigation by the U.S. Attorney's Office, and subsequently contacted the U.S. Attorney's Office on behalf of his client.

The United States brought a civil action against the FAA employee pursuant to 18 U.S.C. 205(a)(2) and 18 U.S.C. 216. The parties entered into a consent judgment in which the FAA employee agreed to pay a $1,200 penalty.

Deputy Secretary of Commerce Improperly Contacts Official at Department of Veterans Affairs

The Deputy Secretary of Commerce received from his father-in-law, the owner of a company doing business with the Department of Veterans Affairs (VA), a letter complaining of delays experienced by the company in modifying its contract with the VA. The Deputy Secretary of Commerce referred the letter to his counterpart at the VA on behalf of his father-in-law, and also contacted the VA by telephone. As a result of the intervention, the company received the modification it sought more quickly than it would have, absent the action by the Deputy Secretary.

A complaint for civil penalties was filed pursuant to 18 U.S.C. 216(b) for a violation of 18 U.S.C. 205. The Deputy Secretary agreed to a civil settlement, including a $5,000 fine, which would have been the maximum fine available under the sentencing guidelines had the case been prosecuted criminally. Section 205 prohibits Federal personnel, other than in the proper discharge of their official duties, from acting as an agent or attorney for another before any Federal agency or court, in connection with a particular matter in which the United States is a party or has a direct and substantial interest.

VA Employee Represents Company Before U.S.A.I.D.

An architect employed by the Department of Veterans Affairs (VA) was charged with violating 18 U.S.C. 205. While employed by VA, the architect represented a Beltsville, Maryland, company in connection with an application for a contract with the United States Agency for International Development in Dacca, Bangladesh. The architect made two trips to Bangladesh to represent the company while employed by the VA, including a trip for which the company paid him $2,090. Prior to the effective date of his resignation from the VA, the architect was paid an additional $5,603 by the company. During this same period of dual employment, he earned $5,540 from the VA.

The architect was charged with violating 18 U.S.C. 205(a)(2). He was sentenced to two years probation, 100 hours of community service, and was required to pay a fine of $1,000. Section 205 prohibits Federal personnel, other than in the proper discharge of their official duties, from acting as an agent or attorney for another before any Federal agency or court, in connection with a particular matter in which the United States is a party or has a direct and substantial interest.

Misuse of Government Resources and Personnel

No Free Government Trinkets

A supervising employee has been forced to repay the Government for giving away property in violation of 5 C.F.R. § 2635.704. The employee presented a local foundation with a unit flag and guidon "as a gift from the unit in appreciation for dedication and support of soldiers who experience and live with PTSD." Unfortunately for the employee, federal rules dictate that US Government employees have a duty to protect and conserve government property and shall not use such property for other than official purposes. In this instance, the flag and guidon were ordered by unit supply and not paid for by private funds. The employee did not seek permission and was apparently unaware that giving away the unit flag without authorization was a violation. The rules are unsympathetic of this ignorance, however, and the employee was required to execute a Statement of Charges for the amount of $112 to pay for the cost of the equipment. The employee also received formal counseling from his Commander.

(Source: Department of Defense, Office of the Inspector General; 2015)

All Your Hotel Points Belong to Me

While working at the Air Force Legal Operating Agency, an official directed Air Force JAGs to stay at local hotels at a higher monetary rate when housing was available on Maxwell AFB at a much lower rate. This official used his Marriott reward points to reserve hotel rooms for visiting military personnel so that he could use his public office for private gain and collect the mileage for himself. As a result of the scheme, the official received a total of 587,282 Marriott reward points and an additional 100,000 reward points for other room arrangements. He pled guilty and was sentenced to pay a $5,000 fine and $90,356 in restitution to the Government for defrauding the Air Force.

An Official U.S-Russian Party

A high-level U.S. military official in charge of nuclear weapons had a real blast on his official trip to Moscow, where he imbibed to his heart's content, mingled with "suspicious" foreign women he met at a bar, and topped it off by insulting his Russian hosts. After a series of other embarrassing gaffes, higher-ups relieved the General of his command. He has since received a letter of counseling and has been reassigned.

Always Read the Fine Print

A former State Department official used her position to funnel millions in government contracting work to her husband's company by persuading a contracting officer to sign the contract without looking at the fine print. How much money was at issue — $39 million — enough for the official to buy a Lexus, a half-million dollar yacht, and nearly a quarter-million dollars in jewelry within two years. The proceeds were going to her company, and she kept secret that the company was owned by her and her husband.

While the contracted work was completed, the 64 year old State Department official was ordered to serve two years in prison for committing fraud against the Government.

I Wasn't Really "Driving" Officer...

An army employee decided to drive some co-workers home after a night of drinking. Unfortunately, the driver had also taken part in the merriment and used a government vehicle. This led to the driver running his vehicle aground on top of a sandbar, stranding himself and his passengers. The driver offered two unidentified individuals a ride in his government vehicle if they helped free the vehicle from the sand pile. Before they were able to free the vehicle, police officers arrived on the scene and arrested the driver. The Government vehicle was impounded the Federal employee was charged with Refusal to Submit to a Chemical Test and Driving Under the Influence, and jailed for 10 days. The employee failed to inform his supervisor about the incident including where he was for the 10 days he was in jail.

The employee plead guilty in state court to Refusal of a Breath Test and was subsequently removed from federal service for driving under the influence, misuse of a government vehicle, loss of driver's license, and attempting to deceive his supervisor.

Pointing and Shooting for Personal Gain

An O-5 in communications decided that his day job wasn't enough, so he started a side business photographing local sports events. While on duty, he asked a subordinate to create photo products for his personal business during official time. The officer also requested a press pass on behalf of the Defense Media Activity, which he then used to gain exclusive entry into sporting events to take pictures in his off-duty time. When he was finally caught for misusing the press pass, he received a letter of concern from command.

Hors D'oeuvres and Wine...On the Taxpayers' Dime

A member of the Senior Executive Service authorized the use of appropriated funds for two optional, off-site "teambuilding" events: a wine tasting event and a hors d'oeuvres tasting event. The SES member argued that these events were justified as "necessary teambuilding" events. It turns out that the events were not so "necessary" after all: no employees were actually required to attend the events, which took place off-site.

The Inspector General found that the SES had improperly authorized the use of appropriated funds for these events, which were not necessary. She was counseled by her superiors as a result.

A Personal Postal Service

One audacious officer stationed in Afghanistan developed a love for fancy rugs and shotguns produced in Turkey. He liked them so much, in fact, that he created his own courier service to get extra cash from the U.S. to increase his collection. The officer, an O-5, submitted a fraudulent courier order, which requested that an enlisted service-member personally transport an "important package" from the U.S. to Afghanistan. The enlisted service-member even received preferred seating on a government flight to undertake his "special" task. When the enlisted service-member arrived in Afghanistan, the O-5 told him that the "important package" actually contained $4,000 in cash for the purchase of more rugs and shotguns. The O-5 needed the money to reimburse people from whom he had borrowed funds to purchase rugs and guns, and to buy more of these items for his family and friends.

The enlisted service-member then sat around on the base for 10 days on his courier orders. When interviewed, he stated that he had received no assignments on base, and spent those 10 days watching movies, eating meals, and doing no work. When the command got wind of this misuse of funds and personnel, the O-5 was relieved of his duties and forced to fully reimburse the government for thousands of dollars.

If the Gloves Fit, No Need to Acquit

A Service NCO admitted to stealing government property while performing duties as a security police officer at a base in the United States. The NCO was observed removing uniform items, flight gloves, and flashlights from an unsecured supply building while making his security rounds. On another occasion the NCO took self-inflating air mattresses and mess kits from the same building. The guard used his police vehicle to stash the stolen goods, before taking them home. The NCO admitted to stealing the items, and was forced to take an early retirement.

It's Five O'clock Somewhere

A government employee attached to a Service base in the United States ended up taking a permanent vacation after a pattern of working an abbreviated work week. The investigation showed the employee worked an average of three hours a day, before leaving around nine or ten each morning to spend the rest of the day drinking at a local bar. The employee put in for retirement in lieu of disciplinary action

Un-Captain-like Behavior

A Service Captain lost his command for abusing his position, committing larceny, and accepting gifts. The Captain coerced the ship's MWR committee to purchase his personal items, for cash, to use as prizes in a command golf tournament. During port visits, he used his position to mandate compulsory wardroom attendance to sales events he orchestrated with specific vendors, in exchange for discounts and free merchandise for himself. At a banquet with an ally military command, the Captain ventured into the other military's Admiral's Mess and removed a pair of ceremonial salt and pepper shakers. Back in port, he accepted a helicopter taxi service and a free round of golf from a non-federal entity in exchange for being a guest speaker, a violation of 5 C.F.R. 2635.202/203/204 (Gifts from Outside Sources). The Captain was relieved of his command.

"I was dozing off – not sleeping!"

A Government employee was reported by his co-workers for sleeping on the job. When confronted, he admitted that he may have dozed off a time or two, but never actually slept at work. His three day suspension was reduced to one day after he revealed that drowsiness was a potential side-effect of his prescribed medication.

Go Speedracer

A civilian reported seeing three Government vehicles traveling at high speeds, tailgating and weaving through traffic in a dangerous manner. When questioned, several service members admitted to driving in excess of the speed limit, passing on the right and driving aggressively. Two of them were given formal counseling on the proper use of Government property and the third was given a non-punitive Letter of Instruction.

Government Parking

The Inspector General received a report that an officer had been using a Government vehicle parking pass to park his personal vehicle while he was at work. The report indicated that on several occasions other employees were forced to pay for parking a Government vehicle because the officer's personal vehicle was using the parking pass. The subsequent investigation revealed that the officer had been using the pass for parking his personal vehicle, and that his superior officers had not been informed or given him permission to do so. Although the officer advised that he only used the pass when going to work, and did not use it when he believed a Government vehicle would need it, he received a letter of counseling.

Government Property for Sale

The Government received reports that a military reservist was attempting to sell Government property, including military backpacks and boots, to civilian employees at a steep discount. The reports seemed to indicate that the reservist had access to a great selection of military equipment because he advertised that he could supply boots in any size that his fellow employees might need. Investigation discovered more than $3,000 worth of Government property in the reservist's home. He received verbal counseling for his misuse of Government resources.

Personal Phone Calls

A civilian employee received a letter of reprimand for her excessive use of her Government telephones for personal calls. The employee had been warned about the issue before, and an investigation revealed that she had spent approximately twenty-one hours of duty time on personal telephone calls to her friends and family over a five month span.

Employee Receives Reprimand for His Side Business

A civilian employee was reported for running a side business through his office. It turns out that the employee had developed a computer program during duty hours and on Government equipment. He then marketed the program, and his consulting services, via the internet. He also used his Government APO address as his business address so that he would be able to handle all of his personal business at his Government office.

The employee received a letter of reprimand and was forced to stop selling the software. Since it was developed on Government time and using Government resources the program was deemed Government property.

Taking the Blackhawk Out for Lunch

A concerned citizen contacted the Inspector General after seeing a Blackhawk helicopter parked in a field behind a restaurant. Inside, he found five service members that had stopped for lunch and were enjoying their meal with several civilians. An investigation revealed that the soldiers were on a training mission, but they had properly listed the restaurant stop in their mission plan. Since the stop was properly listed, the soldiers had not violated any regulations, but they still received verbal counseling because their actions created an appearance of impropriety.

Unwelcomed Whistleblowers

A military service Captain denied reenlistment to a Staff Sergeant on the basis of a protected communication. The denial was based in part on congressional inquiries the Staff Sergeant had filed concerning actions of military officials. The denial violated 18 U.S.C. 1034, which prohibits reprisal against a military member for making a protected communication. The Captain was issued a letter of counseling.

In a similar case, a Captain issued an adverse fitness report after an Ensign had alleged that she had been sexually assaulted by another military service member.

The Ensign had her record corrected after whistleblower reprisal was found under 10 U.S.C. 1034.

Better Call U-Haul Instead

A military service officer used two government owned vehicles to move her belongings from one residence to another. The use of the vehicles, totaling over 250 miles, earned her a memorandum of reprimand from her commander for misuse of government vehicles. Another officer was issued a memorandum of counseling for improperly authorizing the use of the vehicles.

In a similar case, a military service Colonel authorized a subordinate to use a military vehicle to pick him up at his residence and take him to work. He was counseled for improperly using Federal Government resources, including personnel and equipment, for a non-official purpose, in violation of JER 2-301, Use of Federal Government Resources. $130 was collected from the Colonel to reimburse the government for the mileage cost incurred.

Chiefly Wasteful

A chief of maintenance and logistics at a military facility purchased, at a cost of $30,000 each, 6 forklifts designed for inside use despite the fact that the command needed lifts for outside use, even for use in inclement weather. The forklifts rusted for 8 months in an outdoor storage area. In an even more impressive display of waste, the chief purchased a $400,000 patrol boat with a bad generator that left the boat inoperative - and that went unrepaired.

The chief's actions violated Federal Acquisition Regulation 3.101-1, which sets forth the standard that transactions related to the expenditure of public funds require the highest degree of public trust and an impeccable standard of conduct.

The chief was removed from his position.

On-Duty Classes

Two Military Sergeants First Class were handed memorandums of admonition for lack of good judgment for improperly using Tuition Assistance. They attended school during on-duty time when they should normally have performed their military duties.

Their civilian supervisor was also given a memorandum of admonition for improperly allowing the soldiers to take such time.

Significant Penalties for Significant Wrongdoing

A former employee at the NASA Ames Research Center, Christopher Burt Wiltsee, was sentenced to five years in prison and ordered to pay a $25,000 fine after pleading guilty to possessing child pornography on his government computer. Wiltsee admitted to possessing more than 600 images.

He is at least the third person connected with NASA Ames to be convicted of possessing child pornography. Another former NASA employee, Mark Charles Zelinsky, likewise pled guilty to possessing more than 600 images on his government computer. Zelinsky received three years in prison.

Save Your Job; Pay with (Your Own) Cash

A former manager at the U.S. Postal Service was removed from his position for, among other things, improperly using his government credit card and making false statements during the investigation regarding that use. William Hickmon was found to have made personal purchases on his Postal Service travel credit card that totaled over $450. The charges included five gas station charges and an 11-day car rental charge. Though he eventually paid the charges, the improper use was a factor in his eventual removal.

Colonel Finds It's Too Late to Turn Back Time on Unethical Request

An Army Colonel was scheduled to go TDY and asked one of her contract employees to make a reservation for her mother on the same flight. When she was told that such action would be illegal, she responded that it was "alright" and that she had asked him as a "personal favor." After even more people counseled her on the illegality of her actions, the Colonel attempted to stop the employee from making the flight reservation, but it was too late. She was found to have violated Paragraphs 2-301 and 3-305 of DoD 5500.07-R, Joint Ethics Regulation, which prohibit use of Federal Government resources, including personnel and equipment, for other than official purposes.

Cyber-Savvy Teacher Learns a Lesson

A civilian teacher employed with DoD in Japan was caught using his Government computer to send frequent messages on MySpace, Yahoo Chat, and MSN chat during duty hours. He also used the computer to both view and send pornographic material. Students reported that instead of teaching classes he spent most of his time chatting with his girlfriend and family in the United States. Adverse Personnel Action was taken against the teacher and he resigned.

Majorly Out To Lunch

An Army Major was scheduled to work 0730 to 1600 hours. Instead, he would show up as late as 1030 and leave as early as 1200. Somehow, during his short stay at the office he also managed to take "excessive lunch time." He was subjected to counseling for his time and attendance violations.

Prognosis for Army Doctor Does Not Look Good

A civilian doctor working at an Army clinic was caught ordering medication and tests for herself at the clinic even though she was not entitled to medical care by the military. She had also been seen by occupational health providers at the clinic about 20 times.

The doctor was suspended for two weeks without pay for receiving unauthorized medical care – and was retrained on her eligibility to receive medical services.

At Today's Gas Prices, Better Refill the Government's Tank!

A group of interns used a Government rental vehicle to attend a 5-day Defense Acquisition University (DAU) class in Alabama. However, after the class was over they decided to drive to Nashville for a little weekend vacation, ultimately dropping the car off with an empty tank of gas. They charged the Government an extra two days for the weekend car rental and the $5/gallon gas refill. They were also improperly paid for an extra day of per diem during their boondoggle to Music City. The original vouchers claimed days that were not part of the interns' official TDY, but were subsequently corrected. The intern group was counseled, received training on filing travel vouchers, and was made to contact DFAS regarding reimbursement to the Government for the improper expenditures.

A Swing and a Miss for Senior Officers Using Government Funds on Golf Outing

Four senior officials, including two Air Force Generals, a Marine General, and a Navy Admiral, with staff personnel extended their official TDY by an extra day in order to attend a golf outing following a formal conference in Tokyo. They utilized Government transportation and received per diem for the tournament. There were no business events that day, and the all-day golf event was attended by less than half of the conference participants. Attendance at the golf event, costing the Government approximately an additional $3,000, could not reasonably be considered to be official Government business. Golf foursomes do not provide the opportunity to dialogue with a large or diverse group of people and thus do not greatly foster communication between conference participants. The Federal Joint Travel Regulations require that official travel only be authorized as necessary "to accomplish the mission of the Government effectively and economically." The golf did not further any legitimate Government purpose, nor was it an economical choice. The senior officials violated the Standards of Ethical Conduct for

Employees of the Executive Branch (5 C.F.R. Part 2635.704 and 2635.705) by misusing Government property and time. They were directed to reimburse the Government for both the lodging and per diem costs incurred due to the golf outing.

Not a Liar, But the Army Still Can't Train Your Fiancée's Son to Fight Fire

The Fire Chief at an army installation did not have enough students to fill a pre-paid, DoD-funded Airfield Rescue Fire Fighter Class so he sent his fiancée's son to the training to fill one of the unused seats. Although he was not a DoD employee and did not possess any previous firefighter training or experience, he was issued Depot firefighting equipment and sent to the training. This action posed a considerable safety risk to all involved and violated the class's safety requirements. The Fire Chief was not suspected of fraud, only poor judgment. Even though sending the boy did not involve the expenditure of additional funds, he still violated Paragraph 2-301 of DoD 5500.07-R, the Joint Ethics Regulation, paragraph 2-301, in his misuse of Government resources by issuing the boy the Government equipment. The Fire Chief was issued a written reprimand to be made a matter of record in his official personnel folder for a period not to exceed two years from the date of receipt.

Staff Sergeant Tricks Out His Ride on the Government's Dime

An Army E-6 assigned to a National Guard maintenance shop improperly worked on civilian vehicles at the shop and removed car parts for his personal use. He installed truck tires, two solargizers and other accessories on his personal vehicle and used his Government credit card to buy a diamond plate fuel tank and install it in his own truck while putting a regular white fuel tank in the military truck he was working on. The Staff Sergeant not only took a Government vehicle for his personal use, but he even took a shed from the shop and moved it to his home. He was also suspected of using his Government credit card to pay for gas for his personal vehicles. The Staff Sergeant was charged with larceny and wrongful appropriation under the Code of Military Justice and the Government was able to recover $8,800 in property.

Misuse of Position

A Major General and commander in a military service abused his authority by arranging to have an enlisted member serve as his unauthorized enlisted aide. Years earlier, a review of enlisted aide positions eliminated the billet at his center. Despite this, the Major General desired the services of an enlisted aide to assist in official entertaining and improperly assigned enlisted aide duties to a non-commissioned officer. The Major General was issued a letter of counseling.

Law Enforcement Official Fired for Landing Government Helicopter at His Daughter's School

A Department of Homeland Security border officer was fired for misuse of government property after he flew a multi-million dollar DHS helicopter to his daughter's elementary school and landed it on school property. The incident provoked complaints from parents and attracted media attention. Although the employee's immediate supervisor told him he could use the helicopter, the employee's actions were not excused because employees are expected to use their own judgment and should not rely solely on the judgment of their superiors when it comes to ethical conduct.

29-Year Veteran of the VA Loses Job Over Dirty Emails

A Department of Veterans Affairs budget analyst (GS-11) was terminated for the inappropriate use of a government computer system. The employee sent and received at least 119 e-mail messages containing sexually explicit material. The employee had been instructed in the proper use of government computers and signed a statement that he was aware of the agency's policies, which were clearly violated by the contents of his e-mail messages. The employee's claims that someone else got onto his computer and sent and received the e-mails were unavailing.

Don't Lose Your Day Job

A Treasury Department computer specialist used government Internet and telephone service to operate a private business during work hours for several years. The agency estimated that he stole over $63,000 in salary by running his private business on government time. After he was issued a cease and desist order, he discontinued most of his private business activity, but he admitted to continuing to use his work computer to transfer files relating to his private business. He argued that this was allowed by the Department because employees are permitted de minimis (very limited) personal use of government property. The Department disagreed. Although Department employees may use government property for personal purposes at a de minimis level, they may not use government property at all to pursue private commercial business activities or profit-making ventures. This employee had been warned once and continued to use the government's office equipment for his private business. Thus, this employee was left with only his night job (which he could now legitimately do during the day).

HUD Employee Discloses Non-Public Information to Lover for Personal Financial Gain

A HUD employee gave her spouse-like partner information about the minimum acceptable bid required to purchase a HUD-owned property. This information was non-public and gave the employee's partner a significant advantage over other bidders in getting the winning bid. After the her partner won the bid and purchased the property, the property was transferred to the employee for $1—an obvious straw-man transaction used to get around a HUD regulation prohibiting HUD employees from bidding on HUD-owned properties. Federal regulations prohibit employees from using non-public information for furthering their own private financial interests, or the private financial interests of others. The HUD employee was fired.

Block Party for New Staff Members Not a "Hail and Farewell"

A Colonel in Wurzburg, Germany drew the attention of investigators after they discovered that he had used Government resources to host an unofficial barbeque at his quarters. The Colonel had planned a block party to welcome new staff members to his division, and accepted an offer by a superior officer to use Government property and soldiers for the party. He subsequently tasked soldiers from his command during duty hours to purchase food and beverages (with his own private funds) as well as transport and set up a Government tent and Government-purchased tables and benches at his quarters. The soldiers used Government vehicles to transport the party supplies, and returned to break down the tent and tables at the close of the party. While the Colonel protested that the event was a Hail and Farewell, the event was advertised to the community as a Block Party, attendance was voluntary, and the event was not considered a place of duty. Thus, investigators determined that the event was unofficial, and resulted in the misuse of government resources.

Personal Use of Government Property Earns Reprimand

The Assistant Fire Chief at a military installation in California received a letter of reprimand after investigators discovered that he had improperly authorized a firefighter to take home a rarely-used fire station pool table for personal use. The Assistant Chief had been instructed to determine whether the pool table was actually Government property before gifting it to the firefighter, but had neglected to do so. Taking a "cue" from the Chief's admission to investigators, the firefighter returned the pool table to the station and received counseling.

Admiral Under Investigation for Use of Staff to Support Personal Travel

An Admiral's case was referred to the Chief of Naval Operations after investigators learned that he had used his personal staff to book family travel and give him rides home from work. Investigators discovered that the Admiral's Executive Assistant, Aide, and Flag Writer had on multiple occasions acceded to the Admiral's requests to help plan and book family vacations. The Admiral's staff had also booked personal travel for the Admiral's family members to join him on official business. Investigators further found that the Admiral had improperly driven home his Government vehicle on several occasions, and that the staff had developed a custom that the last person to leave the office on a day on which the Admiral lacked transportation was virtually obligated to give the Admiral a ride home in their personal vehicle.

The Admiral's case was referred to the Chief of Naval Operations for misuse of personnel, misuse of Government property, and receipt of gifts from subordinates.

Stopping at the Base Eatery Not an "Official Visit"

A Non-Appropriated Fund Activity (NAFI) employee was reprimanded after it was discovered that he drove his official Government vehicle every morning to a NAFI eatery for coffee and breakfast. The employee readily admitted his actions, but indicated that he believed them to be proper because they were "official visits" to an activity under his command. He noted that he had formerly used his personal vehicle for all such visits, but with rising gas prices, that practice had become too expensive. He further hypothesized that the person who had tipped off investigators was simply jealous as they probably did not have a Government vehicle and were forced to drive their personal vehicle to get food.

The employee received a written reprimand for using a Government vehicle for non-authorized purposes.

Misuse of Culinary Specialists Results in Attention
of Chief of Naval Operation

An Admiral and Captain at a Naval Facility in Japan came under investigation when it was discovered that they were using Culinary Specialists (CSs) to operate an unauthorized Flag Mess. The two officers ordered the establishment of an on-shore Flag Mess to serve them without following the proper procedures to receive approval. While they provided the funds for the CSs to purchase the food for the mess, they required that the CSs prepare meals and serve them in their respective offices. The CSs were also directed to prepare food for an unofficial social event given by the Admiral in his quarters. As a result of their misuse of personnel, the officers' cases were forwarded to the Chief of Naval Operations.

Failure to Choose Cost-Efficient Flights Results in Investigation

An Army National Guard Colonel found himself under investigation after the revelation that he had committed waste and abuse in official travel. Investigators discovered that over a three-year span of time, the Colonel had traveled on twelve flights in business class, adding approximately $6,800 to the flight cost; had taken nineteen trips with non-contract carriers; had on six occasions flown routes terminating in destinations not in his orders, such as San Francisco; and had requested that his staff book him on a certain chain of carriers whenever possible in order to earn frequent flyer miles. Investigators determined that the failure of the Colonel and his staff to follow the proper procedures concerning travel cost comparisons cost nearly $5,000 in 2005 alone.

Trashing Unused Parts Garners Employee Counseling

A Sergeant in the Air Refueling Wing of the Arizona National Guard had the responsibility of properly cataloging excess aircraft parts. This process involved filling out the requisite paperwork and boxing loose items. The Sergeant swiftly became frustrated with the process, and decided to simply throw the items away.

The Sergeant's shortcut earned him counseling and a division-wide review of proper maintenance procedures.

Email Encouraging Attendance at Military Association Meeting Earns Counseling

Two senior officials of the Louisiana National Guard were counseled after sending an email to a large number of sergeant majors in the command asking them to "focus on" the upcoming convention of the Louisiana Army National Guard Enlisted Association, noting that they "expect[ed]" attendance at certain sessions, and expressing their desire for "a good turnout." The email was in violation of DoD Directive 5500.7R, which prohibits official endorsement of non-Federal organizations. The two officers were counseled for their violations.

Don't Let Internet Surfing Carry You Away!

The Facts: The Internal Revenue Service (IRS) issued a policy that allowed the use of the Internet by employees for personal reasons so long as that use did not distract employees from their duties. It also provided a list of Internet sites that were off-limits. Six months later, the Treasury Inspector General (IG) for Tax Administration found widespread abuse of Internet privileges. Abuses included viewing pornographic sites, downloading music and games, and "chatting" online with friends. The IG recommended that the IRS require employees to sign a document declaring that they understood IRS Internet policy and, as GovExec.com put it, "humiliate Internet abusers by publishing their names." The IRS has determined that it will take stronger measures.   *(Source: GovExec.com, June 23, 2003)*

The Law: Different agencies may have different policies as to what use employees can make of the Internet while at work. As an employee, you must follow the policies of your employer or face disciplinary action. Moral: Check the tide in your office before you surf.

Using Government Vehicle to "Chill" Earns Down Time By Suspension

The Facts: A resident of California was puzzled to find a Dodge Ram truck owned by a branch of the United States military often turning up in a residential neighborhood during business hours. Concerned at this use of a Government-owned vehicle (GOV), the citizen decided to give a Defense Department Hotline a call. An investigation ensued, which involved surveillance of the neighborhood in question, review of timekeeping records, and interviews. Ultimately, the driver of the vehicle — a mechanic at a military facility — admitted to having problems with substance abuse and depression and to using the truck at times to return home allegedly to retrieve tools (which could have been obtained by other means) and to "chill out," sometimes for two hours. He admitted that he knew that what he was doing with the GOV was wrong, but he asked for a second chance since he had never been in trouble before. The mechanic was given the mandatory minimum penalty: a 30-day suspension.

The Law: 31 U.S.C. § 1349(b) requires that an officer or employee who "willfully" uses a vehicle owned or leased by the United States Government for other than official purposes be suspended for at least one month or, "when circumstances warrant, for a longer period or summarily removed from office." In this case, the misuse of the vehicle was deemed to be willful, since the Federal employee knew that his personal use of the GOV was wrong.

Holiday Greetings! Military Officer Sent Best Wishes on the Cheap — You Paid!

The Facts: According to sworn testimony and documents uncovered by a military service Inspector General inquiry, a senior military officer and his wife had a subordinate service member print out on a Government office computer official cards containing their holiday greetings, which they then signed, enclosed in official envelopes with printed labels, and sent to about 100 addresses. Some of their greetings were sent overseas to foreign officials using Government postage and marked "Official Business." This conduct occurred as one of a series of alleged offenses that resulted in the officer being relieved of command, issued a punitive letter of reprimand, and ordered to forfeit $1,000.

The Law: 5 C.F.R. § 2635.101 (2003), which lays out basic obligations for and restrictions upon public service, forbids the use of Federal property "for other than authorized activities" (§ 2635.101(b)(9)). It thus barred the use of all of the Federal property employed to produce and to send the greeting cards. Moreover, 18 U.S.C. § 1719 (2003) mandates fines for anyone using an official envelope or label to avoid having to pay their own postage for private mail. In this case, the official envelopes addressed to individuals overseas were improperly used to gain Government postage. Admittedly, section C1.4.9 of the Department of Defense (DoD) Official Mail Manual (DoD 4525.8-M, Dec. 26, 2001) authorizes the use of "appropriated fund postage" by DoD "activities . . . when international diplomacy dictates." In this case, however, the officer's greetings were not required for international diplomacy and were not sent on behalf of an "activity" but were from two individuals — the officer and his wife. They thus did not fall within the DoD exception.

"What do you mean, I can't sell real estate at work?!"

A Federal employee, who had a second career as a realtor, printed her Federal Agency phone number on her realtor business card. When she answered her phone at her Government workplace, she announced her office as "J&B Real Estate." When advised that she could not use her Government office for her commercial business, she left Federal service. The record is silent regarding how much of her duty day was actually spent on Government work.

Sections 5 C.F.R. 2635.704 and 705 of the Standards of Ethical Conduct for Employees of the Executive Branch bar the use of Government property and resources, as well as official time, for unauthorized activities (such as conducting a private business venture).

"What do you mean, this isn't my property?!"

One entrepreneurial Federal employee backed his panel van up to the office door one night and stole all the computer equipment. He wasn't too hard to catch: he tried to sell everything at a yard sale the next day — with barcodes and "Property of US Government" stickers still prominently displayed.

Misuse of Government Resources

Allegations were made that the principal of a Department of Defense school was using the school to hold personal, for-profit craft parties after hours. After an investigation, it was determined that the principal did improperly use Government property. It was discovered that the parties' original location, which had been on private property, was no longer available, so the principal moved the parties to the school.

Section 2635.704 of the Standards of Ethical Conduct for Employees of the Executive Branch restricts the use of Government property, including DoD school buildings, for authorized purposes only.

Improper Use of Government Resources

Allegations were raised that a Navy civilian official was using his Navy office as a headquarters for his private company. It was alleged that he used and published his Navy office phone number as the business's number and used Navy employees to answer the phone and take messages regarding the business for him. It was also alleged that he used Government copiers, fax machines, and other equipment for the business. After an investigation, all of the allegations were substantiated. The official was reduced in grade and removed from his supervisory post.

Section 2635.704 of the Standards of Ethical Conduct for Employees of the Executive Branch restricts the use of Government property, including office equipment and supplies, for authorized purposes only.

Misuse of Email

A Department of Defense (DoD) employee inadvertently received an email message from another employee, whom she didn't know. The message went into great detail regarding a private business venture that the employee was conducting with a third employee. The recipient promptly forwarded the email to Inspector General, who investigated and determined that the writer of the message was using the Government email system for his own private business use. The employee was warned, but continued his activities even after counseling, and was subsequently removed from his position.

Paragraph 2-301a of DoD 5500.07-R, Joint Ethics Regulation, restricts use of Department of Defense communications systems to official and authorized purposes only. Supervisors may allow limited personal use of DoD email systems under certain circumstances and when such use does not overburden the communications system, create significant additional costs, and is of reasonable duration and frequency.

Misuse of Government Telephone

A Department of Defense civilian employee earned the ire of her co-workers by using her office telephone for personal calls. An investigation determined that the employee had indeed been abusing her telephone privileges — for nearly 90 hours in one calendar year alone. She was ordered to pay for the improper calls but was not prosecuted for the over two workweeks worth of time she spent on the phone during work hours. She was issued a letter of caution by her supervisor.

"And they even pay me for doing this."

The Merit Systems Protection Board affirmed the decision by the Drug Enforcement Agency (DEA) to remove a criminal investigator for willful misuse of a Government vehicle. The former official was engaged in a social and sexual relationship with a confidential source of information, who was also the wife of a convicted drug trafficker. The former official received daily gifts from the confidential source. He used his official Government vehicle to travel to the residence of the confidential source, and to transport her from her residence to the Miami airport and to the Café Iguana for purely social reasons. He even gave her some DEA-owned ammunition for use in her own gun.

"Sorry, Skipper, but those really aren't perks."

Immediately upon arriving at his new duty station in Italy, the new commanding officer of the Navy facility, in an effort to save money, used an official vehicle rather than obtaining a rental car, which he was authorized to do while awaiting delivery of his personal vehicle. His use of the official vehicle was discovered when the car was stolen when he was at a restaurant. The subsequent investigation also revealed that he had used an official boat (called a barge) to ferry himself and his social group to the island of Ischia for a social evening (a commercial ferry would have cost the total party less than $20). The investigation also revealed that he had tried to persuade the commanding officer of a subordinate organization to create a GS-14 position for his spouse. The officer was relieved of his command and returned stateside.

Improper Phone Calls and Attempted Cover-up

A General Services Administration (GSA) employee was removed from his position for making 153 non-business calls on a Government telephone to the Texas Lottery Commission. The calls cost the GSA $800. The employee also asked the recipient of the calls to provide false information about the calls by stating that they concerned official Government business. The employee was removed from Federal Service.

Misuse of Government Vehicle

A Department of Transportation canine enforcement team leader was removed from his position for misuse of a Government vehicle as well as for a serious lack of judgment regarding the safeguarding of over $2 million worth of cocaine. The cocaine was used in training sessions for canine enforcement teams. The former employee improperly took his Government vehicle to lunch and left the cocaine unattended – all in a border town where narcotics trafficking was a problem. The charges and the removal decision were all appealed to the Merit Systems Protection Board. The removal was upheld.

How *NOT* to Get Rich Stealing Office Supplies

A Department of Veterans Affairs (VA) review found that a VA employee was unlawfully removing Government office supplies and equipment from the VA warehouse and providing them to his brother-in-law, who worked for a local retail establishment. Management took administrative action against the employee.

Misuse of Government Letterhead and Postage-Paid Envelope

The Department of Veterans Affairs (VA) determined that a VA medical center employee used official VA letterhead as well as a postage-paid envelope to send personal correspondence to a county judge requesting issuance of a protective order against a then-fellow VA employee. The employee was issued a written letter of counseling and advised that future incidents may result in disciplinary action.

Don't Misuse Government Vehicles — Even to Help Your Family!

The Facts: The son and nephew of a high-level Federal employee were having car problems and needed lunch. With what may have been good intentions, this high-level employee decided to use a Government vehicle to help. He damaged the vehicle, and his act was discovered. His reward for helping his family with a Government vehicle: suspension without pay for 45 days and reassignment to a new position.

(Source: Donald Bucknor v. U.S. Postal Service, NY-0752-01-0027-I-2, Jan. 24, 2003)

The Law: 31 U.S.C. § 1349 (2003) requires that any Federal officer or employee who "willfully uses or authorizes the use of a passenger motor vehicle or aircraft owned or leased by the United States Government," except for official purposes, be suspended without pay for a *minimum* of one month and, "when circumstances warrant, for a longer period" or be "summarily removed from office." Moreover, in *Brown v. United States Postal Service*, 64 M.S.P.R. 425, 433 (1994), the Merit Systems Protection Board affirmed that supervisors could be held to higher standards of conduct than non-supervisors, because supervisors occupy positions of greater trust and responsibility.

Misuse of Property Causes Admiral to Lose Promotion

A links-loving Vice Admiral let his love of the game go too far. According to the Inspector General, the Vice Admiral misused Government property, subordinates, and official

112

time to sponsor a private golf tournament—a golf tournament that he advertised as an official event. Tournament participants were rewarded with gifts improperly solicited and accepted by the Vice Admiral from contractors. This led the Secretary of the Navy to withdraw the Vice Admiral's nomination for a fourth star and issue him a letter of instruction and caution.

The Standards of Ethical Conduct for Employees of the Executive Branch limit the use of Government property to authorized purposes only, and official time is limited to the performance of official duties. These regulations also prohibit the solicitation or acceptance of gifts from prohibited sources. The lesson: don't let your activities as a "fore" star keep you from becoming a four-star.

Misuse of Official Mail Leads to Removal

A GS-11 Administrative Services Specialist was removed for falsifying documents and misusing Government property and official mail. The specialist's supervisor had prepared a letter in his personal capacity expressing his disagreement with judicial actions to free the individual charged with shooting and killing his son; this letter was mailed to individuals in the law enforcement community in nongovernment envelopes with privately-paid postage. The specialist took the letter prepared by her supervisor, placed it on Department of Justice stationary, copied the supervisor's signature onto the letter, and sent it out in franked agency envelopes directed to members of the judicial community, the Federal Public Defender's Office, and a law school dean, all without the supervisor's knowledge or consent. The removed employee initially denied having taken such actions under oath, but later admitted that the allegations were true.

As a consequence of the specialist's falsification of documents, misuse of Government property, and abuse of official mail, she was removed from her position and recommended for possible criminal charges.

Use of Government Property for Private Business Leads to Removal

After repeated warnings, a Department of the Treasury computer specialist was removed from his position for unauthorized use of Government property in support of his private business. The employee had used his Government computer to copy his commercial business computer files from one floppy disk to another floppy disk, and computer records showed extensive activity related to the employee's comic book business. A subsequent investigation showed that the employee had falsified his timesheet so that it did not reflect time he had spent running his private business during work hours, leading to an extra $63,000 in payment for work the employee did not actually perform.

Many agencies allow limited personal use of Government property when the use involves minimal additional expense to the Government and does not overburden any of the agency's information resources. Nevertheless, employees are specifically prohibited from the pursuit of private commercial business activities or profit-making ventures using the Government's office equipment.

Misuse of Government Property Results in Removal

A GS-5 employee of the Department of the Interior was removed for misuse of Government property, failure to follow a supervisor's instructions, and misrepresentation of facts on official documents. Investigations revealed that the employee made 1,609 unofficial calls on his Government-issued cell phone at a cost of $752.08, and used his assigned laptop computer to access unauthorized sites. The employee further failed to follow a supervisor's instructions when he charged meals on his Government credit card and used a Government vehicle after receiving instruction to the contrary. Lastly, the employee misrepresented facts on official documents when he submitted a travel document requesting reimbursement for a day when he had not actually been on official travel, and falsely claiming to have held the designation of Agency Representative on three occasions.

The Administrative Judge concluded that the employee's conduct was intentional and that he showed minimal, if any, potential for rehabilitation. Consequently, the employee was removed and banned from seeking Federal employment in the future.

Misuse of Official Vehicle Earns Employee 30-Day Suspension

A U.S. Postal Service employee who used a Government-owned law enforcement vehicle to shop for a personal computer found himself defending his actions before an appellate court judge. The employee argued that the use was "official use" because he sometimes used his personal computer for business purposes; however, the employee admitted to owning a backup computer in addition to the broken one he was shopping to replace, and failed to explain why he could not shop for a computer while off-duty.

The judge was likewise unconvinced by the employee's claim that the use was "official" because he could respond to emergencies while shopping. The judge affirmed the Postal Service's suspension of the employee for thirty days without pay.

Misuse of Official Vehicle, Again

A High Voltage Electrician at the Naval Base in Point Magu was penalized for willful misuse of a government vehicle when he reported to work, checked out a vehicle, and drove to the galley for breakfast. The employee argued that he had never received notification of the restriction against driving government vehicles to meals, a claim somewhat undercut by the fact that he had signed a document the previous month indicating his receipt of the rules regarding misuse of government vehicles. The employee also argued that he was on call for emergencies while eating breakfast, and thus his use was "official." An appellate court judge rejected this claim, finding no evidence that his position as a High Voltage Electrician required him to be "on call constantly" as described.

The judge affirmed the electrician's thirty-day suspension without pay.

Misuse of a Government Vehicle and Weapon Leads to Removal

A series of egregious judgment calls by a criminal investigator for the Bureau of Alcohol, Tobacco, Firearms, and Explosives (ATF) made for eight hours that ended his federal career. The investigator's bad day began when he decided to leave while on duty in order to show a rental house he owned to a prospective tenant, a bad idea made even worse by his decision to drive his official vehicle. Upon arriving at the house, the investigator found an intruder, at which point he decided to draw his service weapon and chase the intruder out, firing a shot in the process. The investigator called the police to report the break-in, and upon searching the premises, the police turned up a second intruder hiding in a closet (presumably petrified in terror). However, somehow absent in the investigator's recitation of the original incident was the shot fired at the fleeing intruder, and the police quickly departed to take the second intruder to jail. Apparently nonplussed at the afternoon's events, the investigator next decided to drive across town (still in his official vehicle) to meet yet another prospective tenant. At this point the police officers learned about the gunshot from the second intruder, and requested the investigator's presence at the police station.

The investigator was charged with (1) mishandling of a service weapon, (2) failure to report discharge of a service weapon, (3) misuse of a government vehicle, and (4) lack of candor. Needless to say, that fateful day was the investigators last in federal service.

Misuse of Government Credentials Results in Demotion

A Supervisory Special Agent, GS-14, found herself demoted to Special Agent, GS-13, after misusing her government credentials in a traffic stop. The agent was riding as a passenger with a friend when the car was pulled over by the police. Although the police officer did not request that the agent identify herself, she immediately displayed her federal credentials when the officer approached. Although the agent never requested special treatment from the officer, the Administrative Judge noted that "mere self-identification by a law officer can result in favorable treatment by another law enforcement officer," and for this reason agents are trained to be careful not to use their credentials for personal gain. The agent was also separately cited for improperly securing her government-issued weapon, which she stored at home "behind the coffee mugs on the refrigerator" because she had "forgot[ten] the combination" to her gun safe.

In addition to her demotion, the agent was also suspended for 14 days.

(Source: 2005 MSPB LEXIS 1812)

Employee Removed for Misuse of Government Computer

The Installation Strategic Planning Officer at Fort Steward was relieved of his duties after it was discovered that he had been using his government laptop to both view sexually-explicit materials and type up notes for his church. The officer will have plenty of time to ponder his actions, as the Merit Systems Protection Board affirmed his removal from federal service.

Lavish Agency Party Earns Federal Probe

On the eve of its two-year anniversary, the Transportation Security Administration (TSA) spent nearly a half-million dollars on an awards ceremony at a luxurious Washington, D.C. hotel. The lavish celebration had over a thousand attendees and was held at the Grand Hyatt, which bills itself as "one of the most magnificent" hotels in Washington, D.C. The ceremony included finger food averaging $33 per person, seven cakes totaling $1,850, and three cheese displays worth $1,500. TSA planners paid an event planning company $81,767 for plaques, which they presented to 543 employees and 30 organizations. Planners also spent $1,486 on three balloon arches, $1,509 for signs, and $5,196 for official photographs.

In honor of this over-the-top celebration, TSA was awarded an investigation by the Homeland Security Department's Inspector General.

(Source: Associated Press, 10/14/2004)

Certifying Officer Personally Liable for Unauthorized Staff "Sunset Cruise"

When reviewing the expense report for a week-long staff retreat, the Veterans Administration (VA) Inspector General noted an interesting charge. Included in the $21,000 bill for the 20-person Florida retreat was an $823 charge for a "sunset dinner cruise." Determining that this item was an "entertainment expense," and noting that the VA's appropriation does not authorize funds for entertainment expenses, the Inspector General recommended that the office director be held personally liable for the improper payment. Upon review, the Government Accountability Office (GAO) found that the "certifying officer" is indeed personally financially liable for improperly certified payments; however, the GAO ruled that the office director was merely an approving official. The GAO ruled that the funds should be collected either from the payee, if possible, or from the certifying officer who actually certified the payment.

Agency Director Suspended for Personal Use of Government Property

A Director of a Defense agency knew of a spare room in an agency warehouse and thought it would be the perfect place to install a bowling lane for a little recreation. However, the employee he recruited to install the bowling alley declined, since he was aware that employees are prohibited from using Government property for unofficial purposes. (5 C.F.R. 2635.704). Undeterred, the Director went to the employee's supervisor and instructed him to issue the order. Reluctantly, the employee obeyed his supervisor and constructed the bowling lane during his official work hours. Perhaps encouraged by his success, the Director secretly constructed another lane.

The Director violated 5 C.F.R. 2635.705(b) by appropriating Government property and space for his own personal use, as well as wrongfully depriving the Government of resources during the time the employee built and removed the lane. This regulation prohibits personnel from "encouraging, directing, coercing, or requesting a subordinate to use official time to perform activities other than those required in the performance of official duties or authorized in accordance with law or regulation." For this violation, the Director received a suspension.

On a side note, the employee's supervisor as well as the Deputy Director/Accounting Director both received letters of admonishment for failing to report fraud, despite the fact that each had warned the Director and even attempted to stop him. As such, it is important to remember that personnel are accountable not just for the actions they take, but also for those actions they fail to take. *(Source: Department of Defense, Inspector General, 2007)*

Senior Officer Misused Staff "for the Government's Benefit"

The Department of Defense Inspector General found that a former high ranking military officer had exhibited a "disregard for the proper use of his staff and for conserving Government resources" when he had his subordinates perform personal services for him during official work hours on many occasions. Violating 5 C.F.R. 2635.702 and 2635.705(b), these offenses include having his subordinates tow his personal boat after business hours and deliver individual family members' income tax returns to a tax assistance office. The officer asked his secretary to research nursing homes for his mother-in-law, arrange personal travel for his wife, and coordinate his weekend golf outings.

The officer also often requested members of his staff handle other various tasks, such as picking up medical prescriptions, laundry, and his lunch. Further, he traveled to a conference a day early in order to play golf with other conference participants as part of his official duties. Section 2635.705 states, "An employee shall use official time in an honest effort to perform official duties."

When asked to explain his actions, the officer declared "unequivocally that at no time did I knowingly violate" any of the standards of conduct. The officer argued that dispensing with these tasks freed him to devote more time to his official duties, and therefore, "the true beneficiary was the U.S. Government." However, the officer's superior disagreed that the golf outing was official duty and ordered the officer to undergo counseling. The officer also had to reimburse the agency for the lodging and per diem costs incurred for the golf outing.

(Source: Department of Defense, Inspector General, 2007)

Morale, Welfare, and Recreation (MWR) Issues

Men Seeking Fines, Extra Duty, and Loss of Rank

Military investigators discovered ads seeking sex that were posted by seventeen military and civilian personnel while deployed to Afghanistan. Among the perpetrators were enlisted, officers, and a non-American. The ads included men seeking women and men seeking men. The ads, determined to be prejudicial to good order and discipline, warranted fines, extra duty, restriction of privileges, and possible loss of rank. The non-American was ordered to leave the country.

The Ultimate Deceit

A military officer was reprimanded for faking his own death to end an affair. Worthy of a plot in a daytime soap-opera, a Navy Commander began seeing a woman that he had met on a dating website. The Commander neglected to tell the woman that he was married with kids. After six months, the Commander grew tired of the relationship and attempted to end it by sending a fictitious e-mail to his lover – informing her that he had been killed. The Commander then relocated to Connecticut to start a new assignment. Upon receipt of the letter, his mistress showed up at the Commander's house to pay her respects, only to be informed, by the new owners, of the Commander's reassignment and new location. The Commander received a punitive letter of reprimand, and lost his submarine command.

Misuse of Government Personnel

Pentagon investigators found that the three-star Army general in charge of the U.S. Military Academy at West Point misused his office by having subordinates perform personal tasks. The General made staffers work at private dinners and charity events, provide free driving lessons, and feed a friend's cat. The General gave each of the staffers $30 and $40 Starbucks gifts cards in exchange for 18 hours of work. In response to the findings, the General paid his staffers $1,815 because the work performed was not for an "official function." In addition to paying the staffers, the General received a written memorandum of concern.

Serving at Volleyball Tournament Was Not Permitted

A Marine Corps Commanding Officer directed, or requested, that his subordinates use their official duty time to perform manual labor and other activities in support of a private organization – in an attempt to fundraise for the upcoming Marine Corps Ball. They worked in exchange for money and command endorsement from the organization. They ultimately received $48,600 in compensation from the outside organization for performance of their official duties, in violation of 18 U.S.C. §209 and Paragraph 3-205 of DoD 5500.07-R, the Joint Ethics Regulation, which prohibits employees from receiving supplemental salary from a non-Federal source for the performance of DoD duties. The Commanding Officer was disciplined and directed to transfer all the money to the U.S. Treasury.

Re-sale of MWR Products

Allegations were brought against a Naval base Morale, Welfare, and Recreation (MWR) Department regarding the printing and selling of T-shirts. The MWR printed T-shirts and then sold them to military members – who then resold them at public events off-base. A civilian businessman who owned a T-shirt business nearby complained that MWR should not be making and selling the T-shirts that were going to be re-sold off-base. After an investigation, it was determined that MWR was not informing the military members about the prohibition regarding the re-sale of MWR goods and was also not informing the military members that they could not re-sell the T-shirts, both parts of MWR written policy. MWR began enforcing the policies and conducted training for all of their staff.

Political Activity Violations

"I'm Uncle Sam, and I Approved this Message"

An O-5 reservist running for state office decided that the usual suit, tie, and American flag pin didn't cut it. He took a number of photos of himself in his uniform, including his unit designators, which he then uploaded to his campaign Web site. He also prominently displayed his rank, position, and pictures of himself on a tour of duty in Afghanistan. While he placed a disclaimer on his Web site stating that the DoD did not endorse his candidacy, the disclaimer was not easily visible and was in a very small font. He received a letter of reprimand after being forced to remove the photos.

Coming to a Mailbox Near You — A Hatch Act Violation!

An O-5 running for state office issued campaign mailers of herself in full dress uniform, and listed her rank in the mailers. She also used her military title in campaign e-mails. In none of these circumstances did she list a disclaimer. When the command caught on, she admitted to the uniform violation and received a written reprimand.

Politics – at Work: More than Just an Impolite Dinner Topic

Two junior Service officers stationed at an overseas base violated the Hatch Act and UCMJ articles when they sent out unsolicited political emails from their government email accounts. The emails supported the President and lambasted other Congressmen whose politics they didn't agree with. The emails caught the attention of a retired military officer, who received the messages stateside. When the retiree complained about the officers using government email accounts for political purposes, the two officers engaged in a scathing email back-and-forth, telling the retiree at one point, "The sooner you and people like you die off, the better." The officers received corrective action within the Service including verbal counseling.

The Military Says Vote for Me!

A Service reserve officer was counseled for using pictures of himself in full uniform on campaign posters, while running for a congressional seat in Virginia. The officer was educated on the impropriety of using his military service affiliation to imply endorsement by a branch of the service. The posters were removed.

More than Politically Incorrect

A civilian employee in a military service sent a mass email to fellow service employees during the presidential election promoting the candidacy of John McCain and opposing the candidacy of Barack Obama. The email summarized a story Senator McCain told about the importance of the Pledge of Allegiance to himself and fellow POWs during his captivity and went on to refer to Obama as a "clown, who refuses to place his hand on his heart and say the pledge." Included in the email was a picture of Senator Obama with other politicians in

121

which only Obama did not have his hand on his heart. The email concluded by saying, "Let's all remember this picture on election day."

Apparently concerned not to leave anybody out, the employee compiled a "to line" of addressees totaling 19 pages. The employee's actions violated 5 U.S.C. 7324, which prohibits political activity while an employee is on duty. For his actions, the employee received a letter of reprimand.

Sexually Explicit Emails Are Not the Only Emails That Can Get You Fired!

Two federal employees, one at the Environmental Protection Agency, the other at the Social Security Administration, were disciplined for violations of the Hatch Act. Although federal employees are entitled to support the political candidates of their choice, the Hatch Act prohibits federal employees from engaging in political activity while on duty. During the 2004 Presidential Election, the EPA employee favored John Kerry, and while on duty, sent 31 of his co-workers an email urging them to support Mr. Kerry's campaign. On the other hand, the SSA employee favored George W. Bush, and while on duty, sent a similar email to 27 of his co-workers and other individuals. It was irrelevant which candidate each employee supported, both were found to have violated the Hatch Act because sending emails in support of any candidate while on duty constitutes prohibited political activity. Disciplinary actions for violations of the Hatch Act range from a 30-day suspension without pay to termination from federal employment.

Passing Out Campaign Stickers at a VA Clinic Ends Federal Career

In his fervor to help elect a candidate for President, a Veterans Affairs employee ignored federal laws prohibiting federal employees from engaging in political activity on federal property — in this case, a VA clinic in Ohio. There the employee passed out campaign stickers promoting his candidate. The employee later acknowledged that this seemingly innocuous act was in fact a violation of federal law (the Hatch Act). As a result, the employee has agreed to retire from the VA. The penalty could have been termination.

Warning: Federal Employees and Some Non-Federal Employees May Not Engage in Politics at Work

The Executive Director of Delaware's New Castle County Head Start Program received a 30-day suspension without pay for promoting a candidate for the U.S. House of Representatives in his official capacity. Violations of the Hatch Act don't get much more blatant than this. The Director invited a candidate to speak to his captive subordinate audience at a mandatory office meeting. The Hatch Act prohibits federal executive branch employees from engaging in political activity while on duty and from using their official positions, authority, or influence to interfere with the results of an election. During the meeting, the Director introduced the candidate, passed out campaign materials, and offered employees the opportunity to register to vote. He later admitted that he had violated the Hatch Act. But why is the Director of the New Castle County Head Start program covered by the Hatch Act? The answer is this: the Hatch Act also covers state, county, or municipal executive agency employees whose duties are connected with programs financed in whole or in part by federal loans or grants. Head Start is one such program.

Agriculture Department Manager Suspended for Hatch Act Violation

A Department of Agriculture manager received a four-month suspension after soliciting political contributions from subordinates. The Hatch Act prohibits Federal employees from certain activities in partisan political campaigns. The employee asked subordinates at work to contribute to the 1992 Democratic presidential campaign. Although the Hatch Act was amended in 1994 to allow Federal employees to participate more in partisan political activities, it still prohibits employees from engaging in political activities while on duty or in any Government office.

Government Employees Sentenced for Political Fundraising in a USDA Building

Four employees of the Department of Agriculture (USDA) were convicted for political fundraising on Federal property. The USDA employees organized a Political Action Committee to raise money for the 1992 campaign. They collected a total of $3,250 in checks from various individuals in a USDA building. To encourage donations, the four employees suggested that contributions to the fund might result in special consideration from the USDA officials affiliated with the Administration. Following the election, the four created a list of USDA employees who should not, in their opinion, receive special consideration from the Administration. The four defendants each received four years probation. Two of the defendants were fined $1,000 and ordered to perform community service. The other two defendants were fined $2,500 and ordered to serve 30 days detention in a halfway house.

Political Activities/Misuse of Government Email System

Allegations were made against a Department of Defense civilian employee regarding the distribution of political material over the Government email system. The allegation was made after the employee sent a political attack message regarding a certain presidential candidate to everyone in the unit—including the commanding officer, who promptly notified the Inspector General.

An investigation determined that the material was inappropriate for distribution through the Government email system. A written memo of counseling was placed in the employee's personnel file. Although the Hatch Act was amended in 1994 to allow Federal employees to participate more in partisan political activities, it still prohibits employees from engaging in political activities while on duty or in any Government office.

Political Activities: Two Humorous – But True – Stories

An election was coming up and one enterprising young Federal employee called his ethics officer to inquire whether it was permitted, under the Hatch Act Amendments, to stuff ballot boxes!

The employee, when told not to wear a Bush campaign button, responded, "But I'm not. This is a button from his dad's campaign!"

Postal Employee Hatch Act Violation

The U.S. Office of Special Counsel (OSC) announced that the Merit Systems Protection Board (MSPB) had concurred with OSC's petition that a mail processor for the U.S. Postal Service's (USPS) Mid-Missouri Processing and Distribution Facility violated the Hatch Act's prohibition on being a candidate for elective office in a partisan election.

OSC's petition charged the postal employee with willfully violating the Hatch Act. The employee did not respond to OSC's petition and instead resigned from the Postal Service on March 5, 2001. The MSPB decision stated that "[name withheld's] resignation does not moot the Special Counsel's complaint. Rather, his total failure to answer the complaint warrants the

[his] removal from USPS." In view of the postal employee's resignation, MSPB required the Postal Service to place a copy of its decision in the employee's official personnel file.

When the postal employee began his job as a mail processor in Columbia, Missouri in 1997, he was given training material that explained that Postal Service employees were covered by the Hatch Act and could not be candidates in partisan elections. The Hatch Act prohibits most Federal and postal employees from running for partisan office. Hatch Act penalties for Federal and postal employees range from a minimum of a 30-day suspension without pay to removal.

Federal Employee Removed from Position for Hatch Act Violation

The U.S. Office of Special Counsel (OSC) announced that the Merit Systems Protection Board (MSPB) had granted its petitions to remove two U.S. Postal Service employees from their positions as Letter Carriers: the first in Jeff Davis County, Georgia, and the second in Nevada County, Arkansas. OSC's petitions, filed with the MSPB in October 2000, charged both men with violating the Hatch Act's prohibition on being a candidate for elective office in a partisan election. Both men had filed papers to run as independent candidates in partisan local sheriff races. Both were warned by the OSC and by their Postal Service supervisors that their candidacies violated the Hatch Act. Nevertheless, when OSC filed its petitions in October, both men remained active candidates and both continued their candidacies until the November 7th general election. Both were eventually removed from their positions in the Postal Service.

The Hatch Act strictly prohibits most Federal and Postal Service employees from running for partisan elective office. It also strictly prohibits state and local employees who have job duties in connection with federally funded programs from running for partisan office.

EPA Official Disciplined for Hatch Act Violation

A Regional Administrator at the Environmental Protection Agency (EPA) in Denver, Colorado, agreed to a 100-day suspension to settle a petition by the U.S. Office of Special Counsel (OSC) alleging that he had violated the Hatch Act. The administrator resigned from EPA in order to run for a Montana Congressional seat, but lost his bid for election. He was accordingly appointed back to his former position as Regional Administrator. OSC's petition for disciplinary action alleged that the administrator subsequently met with one of the remaining Congressional candidates as well as several of the candidate's campaign officials. During that meeting, the participants discussed the administrator's endorsement of the candidate and the solicitation of campaign contributions. Shortly after the meeting, an endorsement/fundraising letter was drafted for the administrator's review and approval. Among other things, the letter stated: "Contributing now to [the remaining candidate's] campaign is absolutely critical." It urged recipients to ". . . make a contribution today."

OSC's petition alleged that the administrator reviewed the draft letter and authorized the candidate's campaign staff to sign his name to it, in violation of the Hatch Act. That Act prohibits Federal employees from soliciting political contributions. Subsequently, the candidate's campaign distributed the signed letter to numerous potential supporters.

The Special Counsel also emphasized that while OSC stands ready to prosecute violations of the Hatch Act, it prefers to help Federal employees avoid such violations. "When in doubt about what is permissible or impermissible under Hatch Act," the Special Counsel advised, "I would encourage employees to consult our office. There's a wealth of information at our website, www.osc.gov, and employees can actually e-mail questions to us."

Five Hatch Act Violations Made by Agriculture Employee

The U.S. Office of Special Counsel (OSC) announced a consent judgment had been entered in its Petition for Disciplinary Action filed against an attorney for the National Labor Relations Board (NLRB) in NLRB's Little Rock, Arkansas office. OSC's petition, filed with the Merit Systems Protection Board (MSPB), had charged the attorney with five Hatch Act violations: (1) participating in partisan political activity while on duty; (2) participating in political activity or in Federal office space; (3) using his official authority for the purpose of interfering with the result of an election; (4) knowingly soliciting the political participation of individuals with business interests pending before the NLRB; and (5) knowingly soliciting, accepting, or receiving political contributions.

Pursuant to a stipulation, the attorney admitted that he had violated the Hatch Act and agreed to be removed from Federal employment. The Hatch Act prohibits most Federal employees from engaging in partisan political activities in Federal office space or while on duty. The Hatch Act also prohibits Federal employees from using their official authority for the purpose of affecting the results of an election; this would include using an official Government title and soliciting "volunteer" services from a subordinate employee. Furthermore, the Hatch

Act prohibits knowingly soliciting the political participation of certain individuals, including those with business pending before an employee's Federal Agency.

Employee's Mayoral Run Violates Hatch Act

When a Federal Aviation Administration employee decided to run for mayor of Albuquerque, he wisely consulted his Ethics Counselor. He was advised that the Hatch Act did not prohibit him from entering the mayoral race. A problem soon emerged, however, when advertisements, press releases, and newspaper editorials started to identify the employee as a Republican, and the employee began to accept financial assistance from the Republican Party. The employee was swiftly contacted by the Office of Special Counsel, which advised him that he was in violation of the Hatch Act and needed to quit his campaign or leave his federal position. The employee, however, took the position that he was not in fact in violation of any laws, and continued his campaign.

Unhappily for the employee, the voters did not afford him much interest, and his campaign never truly got off the ground. He did manage, however, to catch the attention of the Merit Systems Protection Board. The employee's violation of the Hatch Act earned him a 120-day suspension.

(Source: www.fedsmith.com, April 18, 2005)

DC Mayor's Chief of Staff Removed for Hatch Act Violations

The former Chief of Staff to the Mayor of the District of Columbia was forced to voluntarily resign after the U.S. Office of Special Counsel (OSC) charged him with two instances of violations of the Hatch Act. Specifically, the OSC charged that the Chief of Staff — a D.C. employee — improperly asked other D.C. employees to volunteer to work on the Mayor's reelection campaign; the Chief of Staff was also charged with soliciting employees to purchase tickets to a Democratic fundraiser. In return for the Chief of Staff's voluntary resignation and his agreement not to seek or accept employment with the District of Columbia for a period of two years, the OSC agreed to drop its charges.

The Hatch Act prohibits most District of Columbia and federal employees from seeking nomination or election to a partisan political office; soliciting, accepting or receiving political contributions; and engaging in political activity while on duty, among other things.

(Source: OSC, 3/21/05)

Co-Hosting a Political Fundraiser Earns Suspension

An attorney in the Civil Division of the Department of Justice experienced the other side of the judicial process after being charged by the U.S. Office of Special Counsel (OSC) with a violation of the Hatch Act. The attorney had self-reported that he had co-hosted a political fundraiser for seven invitees, presumably unaware that this was a violation of the Hatch Act. The attorney reached a voluntary settlement with the OSC in which he served a 30-day suspension.

The attorney violated 5 U.S.C. 7323(a)(2), which prohibits federal employees from knowingly soliciting, accepting or receiving political contributions. The Hatch Act prohibits most District of Columbia and federal employees from seeking nomination or election to a partisan political office; soliciting, accepting or receiving political contributions; using their official authority to interfere with the results of an election; and engaging in political activity while on duty, among other things.

Political Emails at Work Lead to Employee Removal

An attorney for the Small Business Administration was removed from his position after it was discovered that over a period of three years, he had received, read, drafted or sent over 100 emails from his government computer related to partisan activity. The attorney, an elected official of the California Green Party, used the computer for emails involving issues such as drafts of party platforms, the planning of party conventions, party fundraising, and party recruitment. Although the attorney had previously assured his supervisor — who was aware of his political activities—that he would not violate the Hatch Act, this assurance proved to be deceptive.

The Hatch Act prohibits most District of Columbia and federal employees from seeking nomination or election to a partisan political office, soliciting, accepting or receiving political contributions, using their official authority to interfere with the results of an election, and engaging in political activity while on duty, among other things.

(Source: OSC, 11/28/05)

Humorous Partisan Emails Found to Violate the Hatch Act

During the 2004 election, the Office of Special Counsel (OSC) filed two complaints alleging that Federal employees had violated the Hatch Act by sending politically partisan e-mail messages to coworkers. In the first complaint, the OSC alleged that an employee at the Environmental Protection Agency sent an e-mail to fifteen coworkers that contained a widely-circulated photograph and several negative statements about one candidate. In the second complaint, the OSC alleged that an Air Force civilian employee sent an e-mail while on official duty to 70 recipients that contained a mock resume of one of the candidates.

The Hatch Act prohibits Federal employees from engaging in political activity while on duty, while in any room or building occupied in the discharge of official duties by an individual employed by the Government, while wearing a uniform, or while in a Government vehicle. The Hatch Act does not prohibit "water cooler"-type discussions among co-workers about current events, and consequently does not prohibit "water cooler" discussion over e-mail. E-mail can be used as an alternative mode for casual conversation, but a line is crossed when Federal employees disseminate their message to a mass audience, enabling them to engage in an electronic form of leafleting at the worksite.

OSC has advised that in order to determine whether an e-mail violates the Hatch Act prohibition against engaging in political activity, it will consider the following: the audience that received the e-mail, the number of people to whom the e-mail was sent, the sender's relationship to the recipient, whether the purpose of the message is to encourage the recipient to support a particular political party or candidate, whether the message was sent in a Federal building, and whether the Federal employee was on duty.

No Politics When In Uniform

A military Department chastised two political rivals when their camps ran campaign ads displaying uniformed Marines. The Democratic and Republican opponents in one Congressional District attempted to use the appearance of military support to ensure victory on Election Day, but a friendly visit from a military representative quickly forced them to pull their ads. One of the uniformed men pictured, a veteran, said he believed that because he was on inactive reserve, he could "speak his mind." Military spokesperson pointed out, however, "It doesn't matter if he or she is on inactive reserve," regulations strictly prohibit service members from wearing uniforms in any circumstances that might imply military endorsement of a certain candidate.

Although in such situations the individual services could take disciplinary and/or administrative action, military investigators deemed the service members' involvement honest mistakes.

(Department of Defense, Inspector General)

Two Service Members Posed for Pictures at Political Event

Two service members made a faux pas when local political leaders invited them to attend a "Lincoln Birthday dinner." Under the guise that their invitations to the fundraiser were in honor of their service in Iraq, both service members attended the seemingly harmless event. They soon found themselves in the spotlight, however, when called on stage and presented with a U.S. flag. Although neither spoke at the function, their presence was a clever tactic for special "photo opportunities" used to show military support of the campaign. Posted on the local party's website, the presentation photos violated regulations that prohibit active duty service members from attending political events as official representatives of the Armed Forces.

Regulations stipulate that service members should avoid **any** activity that people may view as associating the Department of Defense (DoD) directly or indirectly with a partisan political event. DoD does permit unofficial attendance at such events but only so long as the attendee is a spectator, **not in uniform**.

Upon discovering the photos, one of the service members immediately took action to remove the photos and alert his chain of command. Because of these actions, and in light of the fact that the party apparently lured them to the event under false pretenses, the two service members received only counseling.

(DoD Inspector General)

Post-Employment Violations
(18 U.S.C. § 207-Type Violations)

Former AF ISR Chief debarred for Post-Retirement Lobbying

The former general in charge of US Air Force (USAF) Intelligence, Surveillance and Reconnaissance (ISR) – has been barred from government dealings. His debarment stems from a three-year USAF Inspector General investigation into allegations of post-retirement rule violations. The general, who aided in development of the US' air strategy during the

Afghanistan and Iraq conflicts, founded a consulting firm upon his retirement from active service and was found to have unethically lobbied on behalf of a client, MAV 6, for a program he had been an advocate of while the ISR chief. The USAF Office of General Counsel (GC), who made the decision to debar the general and his consulting group until February 2016, emphasized that the conduct at issue occurred following his retirement when he contacted several Pentagon officials despite post-employment prohibitions he had been briefed on by the USAF GC office upon his separation.

(Source: AP; published 21 Oct 1989)

Post-Employment "Lifetime Ban"

A Government employee that was involved in approving a contract for audio/visual equipment left the Government to work for that contractor. At the completion of work, the Government had paid approximately $6 million for $841,000 worth of equipment. Several individuals were charged with fraud, and the employee that left the Government for the outside position was charged with violating the post-employment restriction in 18 U.S.C. § 207(a)(1). He received one year probation and a $25,000 fine.

Friends in Low Places

The former deputy associate director of Minerals Revenue Management at the Mineral Management Service of the U.S. Department of Interior (DOI) pled guilty to violating post government employment restrictions. Milton K. Dial admitted accepting a position as a subcontractor working for and representing a company in a contract with DOI approximately six months after retiring from the agency. Before his retirement from DOI, Dial created the evaluation criteria for the bids for this same contract, served on the evaluation committee that awarded the contract to the company, and served as the contracting officer's technical representative at DOI for the company's contract until the time of his retirement.

The company was owned by a friend of Dial's, Jimmy W. Mayberry, who had likewise been a DOI employee. Mayberry pled guilty to a felony violation of the conflict of interest law, admitting in plea documents that he created the requirements for the same contract immediately before his retirement from DOI with the intent of bidding on the contract immediately after his retirement. When bidding took place, Mayberry, not surprisingly, was awarded the contract after he was the only applicant to receive a grade of "excellent" on every qualification category. Mayberry was sentenced to two years of probation and a $2,500 fine.

Dial's sentencing is still pending, but he faces a maximum sentence of five years in prison, a fine of $250,000, and a term of supervised release.

Power Point

A Military Service Captain had, under his official responsibility a program with a government contractor during his last year of service. The Captain prepared a Powerpoint presentation recommending the service contract with this company.

After leaving the service, the Captain went to work for the same government contractor. He was treated to an ethics counseling session after he approached the Government on behalf of his new company and delivered - as the company's representative – the same Powerpoint presentation recommending the service contract with his company.

The Captain's actions violated 18 U.S.C. 207, which prohibits former officers or employees of the executive branch from making (with the intent to influence) communications or appearances before a Federal Government officer or employee in connection with a particular matter in which the former officer or employee participated personally and substantially while an officer or employee.

Federal Employee's Post-Employment Violations Cost Boeing $615 Million, Federal Employee Ends Behind Bars

The former chief procurement officer for the Air Force, who was responsible for awarding billions of dollars in contracts, requested Boeing executives to give her daughter and son-in-law jobs at Boeing. They did, and after the chief procurement officer retired from the Air Force, they gave her a job, too. After a criminal investigation, Boeing admitted to corruption charges involving conflicts of interest and other unrelated violations. Boeing settled with the Justice Department for $615 million. The former Air Force chief procurement officer met with Boeing's Chief Financial Officer and discussed a potential job with Boeing while Boeing was seeking a $20 billion contract to lease tanker aircraft to the Air Force. Federal ethics rules require federal employees to disqualify themselves from participating in matters regarding companies with which they are seeking employment, and federal law imposes criminal liability when federal employees participate in matters in which they have a personal financial interest.

The procurement officer did not disqualify herself from participating in matters involving Boeing as she should have. Rather, she used her position to get her daughter, son-in-law, and herself jobs. She ended up serving a prison sentence for conflicts of interest violations. Boeing's Chief Financial Officer was also charged in the investigation and pled guilty to aiding and abetting acts affecting a personal financial interest. He was sentenced to four months in prison, a $250,000 fine, and 200 hours of community service. In addition to settling with the government for $615 million, Boeing's $20 billion tanker lease contract was canceled.

Conflict of Interest Earns Official One Year Probation

The Chief of the Headquarters Support Branch found herself "fired" after a conflict of interest regarding handgun procurement. The official began employment talks with a company that ran a "reverse auctioning service" for Federal agencies; through this service, the company facilitated online auctions for Federal contracts in exchange for a commission from successful recipients. The official wisely consulted her ethics counselor regarding her job hunt, and assured the counselor that she would disqualify herself from involvement with any contracts involving the company. Unfortunately, the official subsequently participated personally and substantially in a handgun procurement in which she knew that the company had a financial interest.

In addition to attending meetings and making phone calls related to the procurement, the official directed her subordinate to require all prospective bidders to register with and utilize the company's services.

The official pled guilty to a violation of 18 U.S.C. 208 for participating personally and substantially in a particular matter in which an organization with whom she was negotiating for employment had a financial interest. She was sentenced to one year of probation, 40 hours of community service, and a $1,000 fine.

Watch Representing a Business to the Agency Where Employed the Previous Year!

The Facts: A Senior Executive Service (SES) employee of the State Department, who had been tasked with assisting the Bosnian Government in purchasing military equipment and training, retired and within several days took employment with a private contractor of military hardware. Six months later, he recommended to the United States Embassy in Sarajevo that it support his bid for a contract between his new employer and the Bosnian Government. His bid for the contract was successful, but he also succeeded in securing legal action from the United States Government. The employee agreed to a $10,000 settlement in exchange for being released from legal proceedings. *(Source: Office of Government Ethics memorandum, October 2002)*

The Law: 18 U.S.C. § 207(c) (2003) bars every SES employee for one year after ending employment with the United States from knowingly communicating with the Federal agency or office with which he or she has worked, with the intent of influencing that agency or office on behalf of anyone (other than the Government) who seeks an official action.

DoD Official Pays $12,000 to Department of Justice to Settle Ethics Complaint

A former DoD Deputy Inspector General (IG) paid $12,000 to the Government to settle allegations that he violated 18 U.S.C. 207(a)(2) – a criminal statute that prohibits former Government employees from representing others to the Government on matters that were under the former employee's official responsibility during his last year in office. The prohibition lasts for two years after the former employee leaves office. In this case, during the former Deputy IG's last year in office, his audit staff commenced an audit of a particular DoD program. The audit report, which was not released until after the Deputy IG had left the Government, recommended eliminating part of the program that was operated by a private contractor. The same contractor hired the former Deputy IG, who had by then been gone over one year, as an independent auditor to review the audit report. On several occasions, while acting on behalf of the contractor, and within two years after leaving DoD, the former Deputy IG contacted DoD employees and criticized the report with the intent to influence the judgment of the DoD employees.

18 U.S.C. 207(a)(2) prohibits such representations. This statute is often overlooked by Government employees. It includes all particular matters involving specific parties in which the United States is a party or has a direct and substantial interest that were actually pending under the former employee's official responsibility during his or her last year of employment. This includes matters that the former employee may not have known about, or matters in which the employee may not have played in role in determining, but, because of the employee's position, were pending under his or her official responsibility. As noted above, the statute prohibits the former employee from representing anyone to the Government regarding such matters for a period of two years after the employee leaves Government service.

SEC Attorney Sentenced for Switching Sides After Leaving Government

A former attorney with the Denver regional office of the Securities and Exchange Commission (SEC) was convicted for violating 18 U.S.C. 207(a), which prohibits former Government employees from communicating with the Government with regard to matters they worked on as Government employees. The SEC attorney was responsible for investigating certain stock promoters regarding their promotion of stock in a certain company that the promoters owned. Upon departure from the SEC, the attorney was hired by the same stock promoters to perform legal work for their subsidiary companies, including the company the attorney had been investigating while at SEC. The attorney, in his new capacity as director and counsel for the company, responded to a subpoena and communicated with SEC officials on behalf of the company in question.

The attorney was sentenced to one year of imprisonment for this violation of a criminal post-employment statute.

Deputy Assistant Attorney General Settles Post-Government Employment Violation

The Deputy Assistant Attorney General (DAAG) of the Information Resources Management (IRM) office within the Department of Justice left Government service in January 1999. In his former position, he had managed the various functions of the IRM office, which is responsible for maintaining, assessing, designing, and procuring the information systems and telecommunications for the Department of Justice. At all pertinent times, he was paid at the rate of level 5 of the Executive Service pay scale. After the former DAAG left Government service, he joined Science Applications International Corporation (SAIC). On April 7, 1999, now working for SAIC, the former DAAG telephoned the Acting DAAG of IRM. He told the Acting DAAG that he knew that the Department of Justice was considering not using SAIC on a new contract, and stated that such action might require a payment to SAIC, which could, in turn, trigger the Anti-Deficiency Act because budgeted funds would have been exceeded.

The Government maintained that the former DAAG's conduct violated 18 U.S.C. 207(c), a criminal statute that prohibits a former senior employee from communicating to or appearing before employees of his former department or Agency for one year after leaving the Government, on behalf of another, with the intent to influence official action.

Pursuant to a civil settlement agreement signed by the parties in August 2000, the former DAAG paid the Government $30,000, and the Government released him from its claims.

Civil Complaint Filed Against FDA Chemist for Post-Employment Activities

According to the Government's civil complaint, the accused chemist was employed by the United States Food and Drug Administration (FDA) in the Office of Generic Drugs (OGD) for a period of approximately two years. In that capacity, the chemist performed reviews of Abbreviated New Drug Applications (ANDAs) submitted by pharmaceutical companies seeking to gain approval to manufacture and market generic versions of innovator drugs. Shortly before leaving employment with the FDA, the chemist completed the first-level chemistry review of a pharmaceutical company's ANDA for Miconazole Nitrate Vaginal Creme 2%, an alleged generic equivalent to the prescription drug Monistat-7. His review consisted of an extensive analysis of the chemical components, manufacturing process, testing methods, and labeling requirements of the product. Approximately two years later, the chemist commenced employment as Vice President of Regulatory Affairs and United States Agent for the same pharmaceutical company. He subsequently contacted OGD officials on numerous occasions in an effort to obtain approval of the company's ANDA, which was still pending before OGD. His contacts consisted of status calls in which he urged OGD representatives to speed up the process of approval of the application and substantive discussions concerning problems with the application.

A subsequent investigation found that throughout the chemist's contacts with OGD officials, he was aggressive in seeking the approval of the ANDA. Further, the chemist used his acquaintance with supervisory-level OGD officials from his tenure as an OGD employee in an attempt to get special treatment for the ANDA. The ANDA was approved several months later.

In the complaint, the Government alleged that the former employee's actions violated 18 U.S.C. 207(a)(1), which permanently prohibits a former Government employee from communicating to or appearing before the Government, on behalf of another, in connection with a particular matter, involving specific parties, in which he participated personally and substantially as a Government employee. Pursuant to a settlement agreement, the former employee agreed to pay the Government $15,000, and the Government released him from its claims.

Improper Post-Employment Activities by Former Contract Administrator

As contract administrator for the United States Air Force, the employee was responsible for assuring compliance with the terms of two separate construction contracts between the Government and a private contractor. After leaving the Government, the contract administrator was hired by the same contractor, and he became the company's contract administrator on the same two contracts in question. While representing the contractor, he submitted contract progress reports to the Government in order to insure that the Government would compensate the company. Eventually, the former Federal employee submitted to the Government an equitable adjustment claim for approximately $574,613 on one of the contracts. The contract had a basic value of $1.3 million.

The former Federal employee was convicted on two counts of violating 18 U.S.C. 207(a)(1), a post-employment restriction that prohibits former Government employees intending to influence official action from communicating to or appearing before the Government, on behalf of another, in connection with particular matters involving specific parties in which they participated personally and substantially as Government employees.

Pursuant to 18 U.S.C. 216(a)(2), he was sentenced to six months of imprisonment, six months of home confinement, a fine of $2000, and a special assessment of $200.

Air Force Officer Pleads Guilty to 18 U.S.C. 207 Violation

An Air Force Colonel at Eielson Air Force Base worked on the 801 Housing Project, an approximately $70 million contract to build military family housing at the base. The housing would be owned by a civilian developer and leased to the United States. The Colonel was assigned to oversee the project and was the Wing Commander's direct representative. He was also the chairman of the "801 Housing Working Group," which met weekly to discuss any problems arising from the 801 Housing Project. Through his position as chairman of the 801 Housing Working Group, the Colonel worked with representatives of the corporation which took over as construction contractor for the project in May 1994. In October of 1995, the corporation acquired ownership of a second corporation. In January 1996, the Colonel began to express an interest in becoming an employee of the first corporation. He retired from active duty with the United States Air Force during July 1996 and began to work for the company as General Manager, Government Services Division, in August 1996. The United States continued to engage in contractual matters with the corporation with respect to the 801 Housing Project.

In September 1996, the United States and the second, acquired corporation entered into a lease wherein the United States leased from the corporation the military housing units of the 801 Housing Project. Under the lease agreement, the United States was to pay the second corporation $8,688,150.00 on or about October 15, 1996, but did not make the payment until October 21, 1996. On or about the 17th and 18th of October 1996, the now-retired Colonel, as a representative of both corporations, contacted an employee of the Air Force to attempt to expedite the late payment on the 801 Housing Project. In addition, on or about the 19th or 20th of May 1997, the retired Colonel, again on behalf of the corporations, contacted an employee of the Air Force to express displeasure regarding the Air Force's warranty claims on the 801 Housing Project.

The United States charged the retired Colonel with violating 18 U.S.C. 207(a)(1) by contacting Air Force employees regarding the late payment and the warranty claims. 18 U.S.C. 207(a)(1) bars former Federal personnel (civilians and military) from representing another to Federal agencies with the intent to influence regarding particular matters that involve specific parties in which the former employee participated personally and substantially while in Federal employment.

The retired Colonel pleaded guilty to one misdemeanor violation of 18 U.S.C. 207(a)(1) and agreed to pay a fine of $5,000.

Bureau of Indian Affairs (BIA) Superintendent Commits 18 U.S.C. 207 Violation

The Indian Business Development Grant (IBDG) program was created to provide Federal grant funds to eligible Indian persons and Indian tribal organizations. Funds to be released through the IBDG program must be approved by the BIA. The BIA Agency Superintendent for the Crow Reservation was found to have misapplied $103,750 of IBDG funds and $311,275 of Crow Tribe funds for the purchase of land by the Crow Tribe from a private party. The land purchase was never completed. The superintendent subsequently retired from the BIA in 1994 and became employed by the Crow Tribe as manager of the tribal casino. Beginning in 1996, the former superintendent represented the Crow Tribe in appearances before the BIA in connection with the reconciliation and justification for the release of the $103,750 of IBDG funds that the superintendent had approved for the failed land purchase in 1992.

The former superintendent was charged with violating 18 U.S.C. 207, representing the Crow Tribe before the United States in connection with the reconciliation and justification for the release of IBDG funds, a matter in which he had participated personally and substantially as a superintendent of the BIA. He was also charged with violating 18 U.S.C. 371 (conspiracy to convert Federal funds), 18 U.S.C. 641 (willfully converting Federal funds), and 18 U.S.C. 1163 (misapplication of tribal monies) and found guilty on all but the 18 U.S.C. 1163 charge. He was sentenced to five years' probation, six months' detention, a $150 Special Assessment to the Crime Victims Fund, and a $6,000 fine.

Internal Revenue Service (IRS) Officer Pleads Guilty to 18 U.S.C. 207 Violation

While a collection officer for the IRS, the accused was assigned to the collection cases of two IRS taxpayers. After the accused left the IRS, he represented both taxpayers before the IRS in connection with the collection cases to which he had been assigned as an IRS employee.

He was charged with two violations of 18 U.S.C. 207(a)(1), making a communication to and an appearance before an officer and employee of the IRS, on behalf of the two taxpayers in connection with a matter in which the United States was a party or had an interest and in which he had participated while an IRS employee. The accused pled guilty to the charges and was sentenced to one year of probation and 100 hours of community service.

United States Army Officer and Procurement Official Fined $50,000 for 18 U.S.C. 207 and Procurement Integrity Act Violations

The Army Officer coordinated activities for all medical facilities within his region, including Army, Navy, and Air Force facilities. In 1994, the officer retired from the Army and began employment with a defense contractor. This contractor had previously been awarded a contract to provide inpatient and outpatient psychiatric services in support of William Beaumont Army Medical Center; while the officer was employed by the Army, his official duties had included awarding and supervising this contract. The Army Audit Agency subsequently began an audit of the contractor's contract to determine whether an option to renew the contract should be exercised. The audit was completed on January 10, 1994, and forwarded to the officer. On July 12, 1995, a request for proposals was issued by the Audit Agency for a follow-on contract to provide essentially the same services that were being provided by the contractor. On October 13, 1995, the contractor submitted a proposal, which was signed by the retired officer as the company's Senior Vice President.

The retired officer was charged with civil violations of the Procurement Integrity Act, 41 U.S.C. 423(f)(1), and of 18 U.S.C. 207(a)(2), and 207(c)(1). Pursuant to a settlement agreement dated July 23, 1998, the accused agreed to pay the United States $50,000 in exchange for the United States' dismissal of the complaint.

Attorney for Securities and Exchange Commission (SEC), Division of Enforcement Violates 18 U.S.C. 207

In 1993, the SEC attorney was assigned to investigate a group of persons for securities fraud involving the payment of bribes to manipulate the market for the shares of certain companies. These bribes consisted of kickbacks promoters were paying brokers to tout the stocks of their companies. As part of this investigation, the attorney investigated two stock promoters, who cooperated in the attorney's investigation and gave him sworn testimony in which they admitted to engaging in the payment of bribes intended to manipulate the share price of the company's stock. The attorney left the SEC on February 20, 1995 under threat of suspension for unrelated misconduct. He was immediately hired by the two stock promoters to serve as their corporation's legal counsel. In January 1996, the SEC's New York office, working in conjunction with the U.S. Attorney's office in the Eastern District of New York, began an investigation of the entire matter. In February 1996, the SEC issued a subpoena for documents from the promoters' corporation. The attorney, who was then the corporation's counsel and also on the corporation's board of directors, participated in responding to that subpoena.

Investigators charged that the attorney's participation included communications with SEC officials that violated 18 U.S.C. 207(a), which prohibits former Government employees from communicating with the Government with intent to influence in connection with particular matters involving specific parties in which they participated personally and substantially as Government employees. The attorney and five other defendants (including the two stock promoters) were indicted in October 1996 for securities fraud. After the five co-defendants pleaded guilty, the attorney was indicted on a host of new charges, including securities fraud, money laundering, and a violation of 18 U.S.C. 207(a). He pled guilty to three counts, including the 207(a) charge.

Federal Aviation Administration (FAA) Manager Resigns and Then Has Improper Contact with the Agency

While supervising the Airway Facilities Branch of the FAA, the manager had official involvement in the procurement of "Airway Facilities Training Services." This FAA contract was valued at $43,607,755. On March 27, 1992, the manager accepted a position with a bidder for the above-described contract as "Manager, Training Services on the Federal Aviation Administration's Airway Facilities Contract." On August 10, 1992, the bidder included the former manager's name as "Program Manager" in the bid proposal. Members of the Source Evaluation Board, recognizing the name, became concerned as to the possible violations of procurement integrity laws and sought advice from FAA legal counsel. The FAA legal counsel requested an official investigation on June 8, 1993. Evidence produced during the investigation indicated that the manager in his former capacity had personally reviewed, amended, and corrected the Statement of Work for the bid, and had also been responsible for the nominations of two selection board members for the contract. After resigning, the former manager appeared before the FAA on behalf of the bidder, his then-employer, at meetings pertaining to the procurement.

The former manager pled guilty to a single count of violating 18 U.S.C. 207(a)(2), and was sentenced to one year of probation and was fined $5000. This statute bars former Federal personnel from representing a party to Federal agencies, for a period of two years after leaving Government, regarding particular matters involving specific parties which were pending under the employee's official responsibility during the employee's last year of Federal service.

Senior Member of the Board of Governors of the Federal Reserve System Violates 18 U.S.C. 207

Following her resignation, the former Board of Governors member was elected to the boards of directors of a number of companies. One of these companies was affected by a guideline issued by the Federal Reserve called the highly leveraged transaction (HLT) guideline. The Fed requested public comment on the HLT guideline. The company in question submitted a written comment to the Fed, and company officials met with a member of the Fed's Board of Governors. The former Board of Governors member both arranged and attended the meeting. She introduced the company officials to the member of the Fed's Board of Governors, but said nothing during the substantive part of the meeting. The company paid the former employee $1,500 for her participation in the meeting.

The former employee agreed to pay a $5,000 civil fine in connection with a criminal investigation into whether she violated the one-year bar of 18 U.S.C. 207(c), the post-employment activities statute. This statute prohibits former senior Government officials for one year after leaving their senior positions from representing or appearing before employees of their former agencies on behalf of another with the intent to influence them regarding official action.

Former Official at Agriculture's Federal Crop Insurance Corporation (FCIC) Improperly Represents New Employer to Government

A major crop insurance corporation began the FCIC appeal process with respect to adverse FCIC decisions on certain claims (including the case of a certain Maine potato farmer) by sending to the official in question a notice of intent to appeal. Later that year, the official left the FCIC and joined the crop insurance corporation as a consultant. After the FCIC rejected the appeals that the company had initiated, the official repeatedly tried to persuade Agency officials to reconsider the denial of the appeal involving the Maine potato farmer.

The former official pled guilty to two counts of violating the two-year restriction on post-employment contacts codified at 18 U.S.C. 207(a)(2) and was sentenced to probation.

This statute bars former employees for a period two years from representing others to Federal agencies regarding particular matters involving specific parties which were pending under the former employee's official responsibility during his or her last year of Federal service.

Employee Gets Two Years Probation for Improper Post-Government Representations

A contract specialist for the General Services Administration (GSA) pled guilty to violating conflict-of-interest laws after her retirement from federal service. During the specialist's five years at the GSA, she oversaw a number of software-related contracts. She was involved personally and substantially in one large contract in particular, the negotiation of which encompassed the span of several years. Upon retirement from her position at the GSA, the contract specialist sought employment with the company that had received the large contract. Over the next several months, the specialist contacted GSA multiple times with the intent to influence GSA to extend the company's contract as well as award the company new contracts.

The specialist pled guilty to violating 18 USC 207(a)(1), which prohibits an executive branch employee from knowingly making, with the intent to influence, any communication to any agency on behalf of any other person in connection with a particular matter in which the person participated personally and substantially as such officer or employee. She was sentenced to two years supervised probation and substance abuse treatment.

Negotiating with Employer While Engaged in Official Matters Earns $5000 Fine

The Chief of Staff for the President's Critical Infrastructure Protection Board (PCIPB) in the Office of Homeland Security participated in negotiations with a company for a contract to provide support functions for the Board. However, at the same time, he was speaking with the company regarding prospective employment. The Chief of Staff interviewed with the company on July 18th but didn't submit a letter of recusal until July 24th. He received a job offer on July 23rd which he accepted on August 1st. When investigators began to look into the timeline of the employment offer, the former Chief of Staff was forced to step down from the company and pay a $5,000 fine to settle the matter.

Former Admiral Convicted for Violating One-year Cooling-Off Period

A retired Admiral and current top official with a San Diego school district pled guilty to a misdemeanor charge of violating 18 U.S.C. 207, a conflict-of-interest law. As a result, a U.S. Magistrate sentenced him to serve one year of probation and fined him $15,000. Despite previously holding a prestigious Government post and receiving praise from fellow colleagues, the officer's error in judgment cost him dearly. In addition to the probation, fine, and legal fees, he has resigned from the company that hired him, and may lose his job as chief administrative officer of the city school district,

Known as the one-year "cooling off period," 18 U.S.C. 207 forbids former senior officers of the Executive branch from representing other persons before their former agency within one year of leaving Government. In his plea, the former officer admitted to signing a major contract proposal and cover letter on behalf of the company – and sent it to his former employer, specifically with the intent to influence the decision.

On a side note, investigators detected the conflict of interest just in time for the Government to eliminate the company's bid from consideration.

(Source: The San Diego Union-Tribune, July 12, 2007)

Salary for Government Work from Non-Government Source (18 U.S.C. § 209-Type Violations)

Visa Scam Nets $3,000 Fine

The Chief Consular Officer at a U.S. Embassy earned herself a one-way trip to Federal court after investigators discovered she had traded tourist visas for pricey jaunts to Paris and Las Vegas. Investigators learned that after becoming acquainted with a group of businesswomen, the officer accepted several all-expenses paid trips. Two of these trips were to Las Vegas, where the officer and family members stayed in expensive suites at the MGM Grand and Caesar's Palace. Airfare alone for the two trips was valued at $5,000. The officer also accepted an all-expenses paid trip to Paris to attend a charitable event, including first-class airfare valued at $2,400. Subsequently, two of the businesswomen submitted tourist visas to the officer on behalf of various foreign individuals. The officer approved 23 visas, all for individuals who were ineligible under standard Embassy policy.

The officer pled guilty to violating 18 U.S.C. 209(a), supplementation of salary. She was sentenced to one year of probation and a $3,000 fine. No terrorist links were associated with the individuals who obtained tourist visas in this manner.

Charging Customers for Federally Funded Work — Criminal!

The Facts: An Acting Assistant Director for the San Francisco Immigration and Naturalization Service (INS) office charged one alien $950 for a file review (for which the INS does not charge), asked another alien for $300 for an unneeded INS pardon, and charged a third $250 to get a citizen application waiver that had already been approved. The Director was sentenced to serve six months in a halfway house, to be followed by six months of home detention and four years of probation, during which time he would be prohibited from acting in any capacity on immigration matters without permission of his probation officer.

(Source: Federal Ethics Report, Feb. 2003)

The Law: 18 U.S.C. § 209 (2003) makes it criminal for an employee of the Federal executive branch or of an independent agency of the United States from receiving any compensation for official services. For violations of this law, 18 U.S.C. § 216 (2003) authorizes fines and prison terms for up to one year—unless the conduct is willful, in which case imprisonment could be for as much as 5 years.

Navy Employee Commits Section 209 Violation

A U.S. District Court recently sentenced a GS-14 Navy employee to one year of probation and fined him $5000 for receiving an illegal contribution to his salary in violation of 18 U.S.C. 209. In addition to criminal penalties, the employee was suspended without pay for twenty days. The employee was the director of a unit that marketed contracts to other activities and then issued delivery orders to the contractors. While performing these duties, the employee asked a contractor for, and subsequently received, a Coach leather writing portfolio and briefcase and a laptop computer. The investigation started when a contractor employee, who saw the fax that the employee had sent to the contractor requesting the items, notified the Naval Criminal Investigative Service.

Employees may not solicit or accept compensation, including goods or services, from any non-Government source for performing their Government duties. Even though the goods or services may not have affected how the employees perform their work or make decisions, such as whether to award a contract, it is a violation to solicit or accept such compensation.

Senior Official Pays $24,900 Settlement to Department of Justice

To settle charges that he violated 18 U.S.C. 209 by accepting fees for speeches made as part of his official duties, a senior official of the National Science Foundation agreed to pay $24,900 to the Department of Justice in return for dropping criminal charges. The senior official had delivered four speeches to universities as part of his official duties, yet accepted honoraria amounting to $5,500 for those speeches.

Since those speeches were part of the official's duties, acceptance of compensation constituted supplementation of his salary from non-Federal sources, which is prohibited by 18 U.S.C. 209. Federal employees may accept honoraria for activities conducted in their personal capacities, but not as part of their official duties.

Although honoraria are permitted when speaking in the employee's personal capacity, employees may not accept compensation for speaking, teaching, or writing on matters that are directly related to their official duties.

District of Columbia Employee Pleads Guilty to Section 209 Violation

Several inspectors employed by the District of Columbia Department of Consumer and Regulatory Affairs were accepting bribes and gratuities in exchange for the issuance of construction, plumbing, and electrical permits. In one instance, a private architect paid "tips" to one of these inspectors in exchange for speedy and favorable inspections on his renovation projects. The architect was allowed to plead guilty to a misdemeanor count of section 209, and was sentenced to one year of probation and a $1,000 fine. The inspectors were convicted on charges of violating 18 U.S.C. 201 (Bribery).

18 U.S.C. 209 bars the unlawful supplementation of salary and applies to officers and employees of the District of Columbia and non-Government sources who compensate any such officers and employees for their Government services.

District of Columbia DMV Employee Pleads Guilty to Section 209 Charge

An employee of the District of Columbia Department of Motor Vehicles (DMV) was caught accepting bribes in exchange for altering DMV computer records in order to "clean up" the driving records of individuals who had outstanding traffic tickets or past violations that might prevent them from obtaining a driver's license. These bribe transactions were arranged through a middleman. The DMV employee and the middleman were convicted of violating 18 U.S.C. 209; the DMV employee was sentenced to two years probation and a $200 fine, and the middleman was sentenced to one-year probation and a $250 fine. Two citizens who paid the parties to get their records "cleaned up" were convicted of violating 18 U.S.C. 201 (bribery). 18 U.S.C. 209 bars the unlawful supplementation of salary and applies to Federal officers and employees as well as those of the District of Columbia and non-Government sources who compensate any such officers and employees for their Government services.

Private Citizen Attempts to Bribe Internal Revenue Service (IRS) Employee

The citizen tried to bribe the IRS employee by paying him $250 for favorable treatment regarding an IRS matter. The citizen pled guilty to a misdemeanor violation of 18 U.S.C. 209, which prohibits the payment of supplementation to a Government employee's salary.

Civilian Employee at Langley Air Force Base in Virginia Violates 18 U.S.C. 209

An Air Force employee was designated by his Agency as the supervisory construction representative for the Simplified Acquisition of Base Engineering Requirements (SABER) contract. Under this contract, a private company agreed to provide base engineering and construction services at Langley Air Force Base. The prime contractor subcontracted its electrical work to another company. A supervisor with the subcontractor subsequently provided the Air Force employee with an air conditioning system, a Jet Ski and trailer, a home computer system, and a laptop computer, with a total value of approximately $16,500.

The Air Force employee pled guilty to a misdemeanor violation of 18 U.S.C. 209, for receiving a supplementation to his salary as compensation for his services as a Government employee. He was sentenced to three years probation and a $2500 fine.

Central Intelligence Agency (CIA) Employee Drives Overseas Auto Scheme

As a U.S. Federal employee residing in Egypt, the employee discovered that he could purchase an imported vehicle in Egypt without having to pay the normal 150% excise tax. This fact had created a black market in which Egyptian car brokers would pay U.S. employees to register luxury cars in their names in order to allow the dealers to evade import taxes. Investigators found that while in Cairo, Egypt, the employee had agreed to accept $25,000 in exchange for changing the status of his personally-owned vehicle with the Egyptian Ministry of Foreign Affairs, which would allow him to participate in the scheme.

The CIA employee was convicted of violating 18 U.S.C. 209 and was sentenced to six months' supervised release, six months' home detention, and 200 hours of community service.

(Source: OGE 1998 Conflict of Interest Prosecution Survey)

Family Business Venture Ends in Violation of 18 U.S.C. 209

A contracting officer at the Naval Surface Warfare Center started a computer equipment business with his father-in-law to provide extra income. The duo concocted a scheme whereby the contracting officer steered Government contracts for the purchase of computer equipment to the father-in-law, who would buy the equipment from a third party vendor through a computer supply magazine. The two would then overcharge the Government and split the profit. This netted a payment of $29,000 for $11,000 worth of computer equipment. Both parties split the $18,000 overcharge.

The father-in-law pled guilty to a misdemeanor violation of 18 U.S.C. 209, which prohibits the supplementation of a Government employee's salary, and the contracting officer pled guilty to wire fraud and mail fraud. In their pre-indictment plea agreements, the father-in-law agreed to pay $18,000 restitution, and the contracting officer agreed to pay an amount of restitution to be determined at the sentencing hearing.

Cab Company Owner and District of Columbia Official Conspire to Violate 18 U.S.C. 209

Suspicious investigators discovered that for three years, a cab company owner had conspired with the Chief of the D.C. Office of Taxicabs to provide illegal taxicab driver's licenses to unqualified drivers. The drivers paid money to the company owner, who took the money and the drivers' names to the D.C. official. The official then prepared the illegal licenses. The company owner also paid the D.C. official money for other illegal favors, such as registering vehicles that should not have been registered.

The D.C. official pled guilty to violating 18 U.S.C. 209, which prohibits the supplementation of a Government employee's salary, and agreed to testify against the cab company owner. The D.C. official was also convicted of nine felony counts, including accepting bribes and gratuities in violation of 18 U.S.C. 201.

Air Force Contracting Officer Pays $6000 for 18 U.S.C. 209 Violation

In return for favorable treatment in contracting, employees of a private company agreed to provide an Air Force contracting officer with money in the form of condominium rental payments. That money was paid through different intermediaries in order to disguise the purpose and the source of the funds. In addition, an investigation disclosed that the company purchased certain valuable goods and items for the condominium. Finally, the investigation disclosed that the company purchased smaller value items, such as dinners and basketball tickets, for the Air Force contracting officer. Due to statute of limitations problems, the investigation focused on the payment of the smaller value items.

The contracting officer pled guilty to a single misdemeanor count of 18 U.S.C. 209, unlawfully augmenting his salary while employed by the Air Force. He was ordered to pay a fine of $6,000, which the Court calculated to be three times the value of those accepted items.

Payoff for Special Access at Government Auction Ends in $1000 Fine

In an attempt to gain preferential treatment at a Government auction, two brothers paid off an auction guard. Instead, they wound up purchasing misdemeanor violations of 18 U.S.C. 209 (supplementation of a Government employee's salary). Sentences of probation and a $1,000 fine were imposed on each.

Assistant United States Attorney (AUSA) in Tucson Illegally Possesses Sheep Skull and Horns

The Assistant U.S. Attorney prosecuted an individual for illegally killing a bighorn sheep on an Indian Reservation. As a result of the prosecution, the hunter forfeited the bighorn sheep and trophy (skull and horns), valued at approximately $5,000, to the Arizona Game and Fish Department. Pursuant to a request from the AUSA, the Arizona Game and Fish Department entered into an agreement with the AUSA allowing him to publicly display the skull and horns in his office, but requiring their return upon request. However, after leaving employment with the U.S. Attorney's office, the AUSA took the skull and horns with him and treated them as his personal property. When the former AUSA was questioned a year later about his possession of the skull and horns, he claimed that an unspecified Indian had sent the skull and horns to him in appreciation for his work on the prosecution of the hunter. Investigation showed that such a gift would have been contrary to tribal practices and no member of the tribe could be found who knew anything about the alleged gift.

The Government then regained possession of the skull and horns from the former AUSA and returned them to the tribe. The AUSA agreed to plead guilty to violating 18 U.S.C. 209 for his possession of the trophy.

Secretary at Federal Prison Pleads Guilty to 18 U.S.C. 209 Violation

Investigators discovered that the secretary at a Federal prison had accepted money from an inmate in exchange for allowing him certain privileges, including allowing him to place unauthorized calls on her office phone. The defendant pled guilty to the charge of receiving compensation from a non-Government source for doing her Government job (18 U.S.C. 209(a)) and was sentenced to two years probation.

Postal Service Employee Convicted of 18 U.S.C. 209 Violation

Investigators discovered that an assistance counselor with the Postal Service was taking kickbacks from a nearby hospital. The counselor provided assessment, referral, and follow-up counseling services to Postal Service employees and their families relating to chemical dependency or behavioral problems. While performing these duties, the counselor received cash, a telephone credit card, limousine services, food, hotel accommodations, and travel reimbursement for himself, his wife and his brother from a Topeka, Kansas hospital. These benefits had an aggregate value of in excess of $45,000. The hospital was a psychiatric care and drug-alcohol dependency treatment facility.

The counselor was charged with fifteen counts of violating 18 U.S.C. 209, for accepting dual compensation, and pled guilty.

GSA Employee Convicted of Violating 18 U.S.C. 209

As the Comptroller of the General Services Administration (GSA), the employee in question was responsible for implementing and overseeing GSA's contract with Diners Club for Government charge cards. During the life of the contract, the employee accepted numerous expensive meals from Diners Club employees in Washington, D.C., as well as accommodations, meals, and entertainment in Las Vegas and Phoenix.

The employee pled guilty to one count of conspiracy (18 U.S.C. 371) and one count of receiving dual compensation (18 U.S.C. 209), both misdemeanors. He was sentenced to one year of supervised probation and a $250 fine.

150

Citizen Pleads Guilty to Violating 18 U.S.C. 209

A private electrical contractor was charged with supplementing the salary of a Public Affairs Officer who was a representative for small and disadvantaged businesses for the Army Corps of Engineers. The contractor was involved in the payment of money to the officer in return for the officer's assistance in facilitating the sale and development of land for off-post housing around Fort Drum, New York.

The contractor pled guilty to violating 18 U.S.C. 209, supplementing the salary of a Federal employee, and was sentenced to one year of probation.

Public Works Employee "Gets the Boot" for Accepting Payments

An employee of the Vehicle Immobilization Branch at the D.C. Department of Public Works who decided to supplement his salary with private funds quickly found himself with no salary at all. The employee solicited and accepted $400 in cash for removing a lawfully-attached boot on a D.C. vehicle. In return, the employee received three years probation, six months home detention, 100 hours community service, and $300 in fines for his violation of 18 U.S.C. 209, illegal supplementation of salary.

Easy Come, Easy Go

Investigators discovered that an Immigration and Naturalization Service Adjudication Officer had taken bribes from an immigration consultant to facilitate the consultant's cases. The officer pled guilty to three misdemeanor counts of violating 18 U.S.C. § 209(a), receiving compensation from a private party for services rendered to the United States.

Accepting Bribes for Priority Service Earns $10,000 Fine

A Veterans Affairs rating assistant technician responsible for prepping claims files for adjudication was found to have taken bribes from filers to green-light false and inflated disability claims for review. He pled guilty to one felony count of violating 18 U.S.C. § 209 (a), unlawfully accepting supplementation of government salary, and was slapped with four years probation, $10,000 in fines, and 120 hours of community service.

Gifts from Vendor Result in Two Years Probation

An employee of the Department of the Interior's Office of the Geological Survey took advantage of her government charge card responsibilities and started accepting gift cards from a certain vendor in return for steering her purchases his way. Her $500 in gift cards cost her two years of probation and 100 hours of community service when she pled guilty to one count of violating 18 U.S.C. § 209, unlawfully accepting supplementation of her government salary.

Time and Attendance Violations

Travel Fraud

A government employee temporarily promoted to fill an organization's directorship position has been fired for misconduct related to travel. As part of his assignment, the employee, who was stationed on the east coast, was authorized travel to his temporary unit located on the west coast. During his directorship tenure, the employee twice flew home on TDY orders to the east coast for the purpose of taking leave. Regulations permit personal leave to be taken in conjunction with TDY travel, but the travel must not be for the purpose of taking leave. There must be a driving mission requirement for the travel. The employee, upon being confronted about the legality of the TDY orders, stated that he had conducted official business while back on the east coast. The evidence established otherwise, and investigators substantiated the allegations of improper travel. In response to these substantiated findings, the employee's temporary assignment on the east coast was terminated and he was immediately directed to return to home station. TDY money accrued during the employee's travel was recouped and a letter of requirement was issued to him outlining his violations and directing subsequent compliance. Probably the worse outcome for the employee, however, was foreclosing the opportunity to convert this temporary promotion into a permanent promotion had it gone well.
(Source: Department of Defense, Office of the Inspector General; 2015)

Contractor On-The-Clock Outside Employment

A government contractor has been fired for running a personal landscaping business while being paid by the government during duty hours. Co-workers heard telephone discussions pertaining to his business placed from his government telephone and he was found using government printers to print advertising materials. Upon hearing of the misconduct, the contract company took swift action in terminating the official upon the conclusion of its own investigation. The Government, however, is expected to continue pursuing all contract remedies as a result of this misconduct, including reimbursement for overpayment of time charged by the contract for work not performed.

(Source: Department of Defense, Office of the Inspector General; 2015)

Employee T-Shirt Business

According to government rules, supervisors are not permitted to solicit from subordinates. One supervisor recently found herself the scope of an agency inquiry into this provision – when subordinates inquired into her personal t-shirt and vitamin business. Despite not "directly" engaging subordinates to buy her merchandise – and only fielding unprompted inquiries from them about the prospect of purchasing her products – sales resulted and this was deemed a violation of the rules given that the sales could have easily compromised her position of authority.

5 C.F.R. § 2635.705 also regulates the use of government time. Notwithstanding being a long term employee with six years of supervisor experience, the supervisor was unaware that conducting personal business during official work hours is prohibited. While all transactions were conducted during breaks, some of them took place within the building and it was deemed to not promote the intent of the law by selling during breaks. The supervisor was found to have executed poor judgment and should have inquired as to the legality of selling merchandise and conducting business at work. Possible repercussions of her actions could have included creating conflicts of interest – negatively affecting office productivity or the tone of the workplace.

As a result of her conduct, the agency director required training be conducted on regulatory guidance regarding solicitation in the workplace.

(Source: Department of Defense, Office of the Inspector General; 2015)

College Work On-The-Clock

A supervisor and subordinate have been disciplined for college work done while on the government clock. The subordinate, going to school part-time while working as a federal employee, was allowed by his supervisor to work on homework on his government computer while on duty. In fact, binders, textbooks, and course syllabus were observed open such that witnesses testified that the subordinate was "completely engaged" during the one to eight hours a day he was working on his courses. Computer records substantiated this testimony, noting a number of unofficial, educational, or sports related websites being visited during duty hours. Additionally, the supervisor had been approached on a number of occasions about the subordinate's use of time. He took no action, however, allowing the subordinate to continue. As a result of this conduct, both individuals were counseled on appropriate use of the subordinate's time. Also, all personnel in that office were trained on acceptable use of government communications equipment and the supervisor was directed to more closely monitor the subordinate's use of time and government equipment.

(Source: Department of Defense, Office of the Inspector General; 2015)

Secret Agent Man?

A former high-level official at the Environmental Protection Agency (EPA) stole nearly $900,000 from the Government by pretending to be part of a detail to the Central Intelligence Agency (CIA) for nearly two decades. He duped a series of supervisors, including top officials, by disappearing from the office and explaining his absences by telling his bosses that he was doing top-secret work for the CIA and its "directorate of operations." No one at EPA ever checked to see if he worked for the CIA. In all, he was paid for 2.5 years of work that he did not perform and received about $500,000 in "retention bonuses" that he did not deserve. In addition, he lied about contracting malaria, which cost the EPA $8,000 over three years for a parking space reserved for the disabled. He was reimbursed for $57,000 in fraudulent travel expenses, and he continued to draw a paycheck for 19 months after his retirement.

He has repaid the nearly $900,000 to the EPA, but still owes $507,000 in a money judgment. He was sentenced to 32 months in prison.

A Few Unexcused Absences

An employee of a military service was not particularly careful about his time reporting. The employee arrived late, left early, and left the building for extended periods of undocumented time. Of 289 workdays reviewed during an investigation, the employee was found to have worked less than the required 8.5 hours on 135 occasions (47% of the time); all told, the employee misstated his work hours by over 100 hours.

For his unscrupulous timekeeping, the employee received a letter of reprimand and was charged leave to accurately reflect his attendance.

In a similar case, an employee of a DoD facility was issued a letter of warning and instruction after she arrived late on several days but left at the scheduled shift completion time without claiming leave or reporting her tardiness to management.

The letter instructed the employee to sign-in and sign-out. Notwithstanding the letter, it was later determined that the employee continued to fail to fulfill her time commitments, leaving over an hour early on multiple occasions.

The employee was issued a letter of reprimand for leaving the worksite without permission.

DVD Bootleggers MIA During Government Work Hours

A Federal employee used his Government computer to make illegal copies of commercial DVDs in violation of copyright laws. He and another employee also used their Government computers and duty time to watch the movies. The other employee took lunches lasting up to three hours in order to watch the DVDs and take naps. Initially the employees' supervisors signed off on this behavior, even assigning extra work to others to make up for the employees' time wasted napping and movie watching. The employee who copied the DVDs received a written reprimand. The supervisor received an oral admonishment for failing to address the misconduct, and another employee received a Letter of Counseling for knowingly accepting a pirated DVD. In a similar case, a civilian employee working for the U.S. Army in Germany was involved in selling pirated DVDs. He used the profits from his illegal operation to buy vacation homes and luxury cars and to pay for frequent European ski vacations. He devoted some of his duty time to the marketing and selling of the bootleg videos, including taking payments while on the job.

Even though the employee had left Federal service by the time the accusations against him were substantiated, administrative action was taken to bar him from US Army Europe installations.

Out-of-Office Reply: Out Sick: Can be Reached at Bowling Alley

A GS-14 Director, within an Army Command, failed to show up to work for at least three months. He complained of needing a double hip replacement but never submitted sick leave. Though he claimed to work from home, he was never approved for a work-at-home program. People reported seeing him around the community and he was spotted at the PX, the Commissary, and even the bowling alley! The man received a verbal reprimand and was counseled on appropriate leave request and approval procedures.

Falsification of Time Cards Results in Removal

An employee at the Walter Reed Army Medical Center had a habit of showing up for work only one week a month. However, her supervisor soon noticed that the employee's paycheck did not reflect this erratic schedule. Upon questioning, the employee admitted to changing the pay codes on her time card after they were signed by her supervisor.

The employee was allowed to resign, and is indebted to the Government for $10,383.47. The money will be deducted from her retirement pay.

Pre-signing Employee's Time Card Results in Counseling

An Air Force Sergeant at the Field Maintenance center pre-signed one of her subordinate's time cards before she left for a two-week leave. Unfortunately for her, the subordinate subsequently changed several of the boxes she had originally marked as "leave" to "regular flex time," and then took leave while still drawing regular pay. When investigators discovered the discrepancy, the subordinate resigned. The trusting Sergeant earned counseling for failing to comply with DoD Financial Management Regulations, which stipulate that supervisors must correctly certify time cards at the end of the pay period in order to prevent employee fraud.

Lying About Overtime Doesn't Pay!

The Facts: A former employee of the Department of Defense entered overtime hours he hadn't worked into a computer time-keeping system. He was caught. He pleaded guilty and was ordered to pay the Government $7,500 and was sentenced to three years probation — not the sort of overtime he was looking for.   *(Source: Federal Ethics Report, Apr. 2003)*

The Law: 18 U.S.C. § 287 (2003) states that anyone presenting to any "person or officer in the civil, military, or naval service of the United States, or to any department or agency thereof" a claim for money from the Federal Government, knowing such claim to be false, shall be fined and imprisoned for no more than 5 years.

Hung By Wire Fraud

The Facts: A Defense Intelligence Agency secretary in Arlington, Virginia, improperly obtained access to her time and attendance records on 74 occasions. She used her access to credit herself with over 4,000 hours of overtime she hadn't worked. She was caught and pleaded guilty to wire fraud, for which she was sentenced to twelve months and one day in prison, to be followed by three years of probation with participation in Gamblers Anonymous. She also had to pay the Government $91,380 in restitution. Hopefully, she learned from this bad bet.

(Source: Federal Ethics Report, Apr. 2003)

The Law: 18 U.S.C. § 1343 (2003) mandates penalties for transmitting "by means of wire, radio, or television communication in interstate or foreign commerce, any writings, signs, signals, pictures, or sounds" in order to execute a plan to defraud. The penalties: Fines, imprisonment of not more than 20 years, or both — unless the fraud affects a financial institution, in which case the fine is to be of not more than $1 million and the imprisonment of not more than 30 years.

Falsifying Overtime Can Be a Costly Business

The Facts: A Federal employee at the Pentagon decided to participate in a scheme that involved logging false overtime hours in an electronic timekeeping system. The employee pled guilty at trial and was sentenced to three years of probation along with six months of home confinement, and ordered to pay over $16,000 restitution.

(Source: Federal Ethics Report, March 2003)

The Law: 18 U.S.C. § 287 (2003) mandates fines and imprisonment for up to five years for anyone who presents a claim for money, which the person knows to be fraudulent, to the "civil, military, or naval service of the United States."

Improper Time Sheets

Allegations were made that a Department of Defense (DoD) employee was not working his assigned hours and was fraudulently claiming overtime hours he did not work. After an investigation, it was determined that the employee was attending college courses at lunch for approximately two hours and worked late to make up the time. His time and attendance sheets showed him working his normal hours with no indication of the long lunch and late hours to accommodate his college courses. The sheets were submitted without showing the modified schedule because a clerk incorrectly told the employee's supervisor that "the system wouldn't allow variations from a normal workday." The employee, the supervisor, and the clerk were all instructed on proper timekeeping procedures.

INS Grants Administrative Leave as Award for Contributions to CFC

Officials in an Immigration and Naturalization Service (INS) district office rewarded employees who contributed at least $500 to the Combined Federal Campaign (CFC) with eight hours of administrative leave. After an investigation, it was found that the employees who were granted and used the leave did not have the leave properly documented on their time sheets. As the district director did not carry out the violations in a knowing and willful way and because the employees affected stated they did not feel coerced, no charges were filed. The director did receive a letter of counseling regarding her management of the CFC program, however.

VA Physician Time and Attendance Issue

An administrative investigation substantiated that a part-time Department of Veterans Affairs (VA) physician routinely worked at a non-VA clinic during his VA core hours and as a result failed to meet his VA tour of duty obligation. The investigation also revealed that the physician's supervisor failed to check on him to ensure that he was working the hours required. In response to the investigator's recommendation, administrative action was taken against both the physician and the supervisor. The physician was charged leave for the hours not worked and was instructed to revise his hours at the non-VA clinic.

Employees Terminated for Abusing Religious Leave

For a period of several years, two top executives at the Naval Undersea Warfare Center had an astonishing work record — they took nearly no vacation time at all. The reason, investigators soon discovered, was that the executives had been taking "religious compensatory time" instead. Curiously, the executives' absences seldom fell on any traditionally-observed religious holidays. Instead, investigators found that the pair's so-called religious observances took place on days when they had medical appointments, sightseeing trips, and golf tournaments. Asked whether golf tournaments could be considered religious observances, one executive replied, "They could be for some people."

Unamused, the Inspector General found that the two had made a "premeditated, conspiratorial effort to defraud the Government," and forced them into retirement. Religious compensatory time is available for government employees who need to observe religious requirements – but even then, it needs to be made up at a later time.

(Source: www.GovExec.com, July 1, 2004)

Use of Sick Leave for Military Tours Earns Employee Dismissal

A reservist's use of sick leave to account for absences on active-duty military tours resulted in the end of a 20-year federal career. Over a period of several years, the reservist accounted for absences from his civilian position at CENTCOM as "sick leave," when in fact he was on active-duty military tours. This allowed the employee to bank annual leave, as well as collect dual salaries from both the civil service and the military. Given the reservist's two decades of federal employment, the judge found the reservist's pleas of ignorance as to the proper leave procedures unconvincing. The judge also took into consideration the testimony of the reservist's commanding officer at CENTCOM, who testified that his trust in the reservist had been wholly eroded.

As a consequence of the reservist's abuse of the leave system, his career in the civil service was terminated.

(Source: 2005 MSRP LEXIS 6041)

Disciplined for Double Counting Civilian and Military Reserve Duties

A senior agency attorney did a little "double duty," and as a "reward," he was ordered to reimburse the agency for 500.5 hours of annual leave and 18 hours of sick leave. The agency report found the lawyer spent the equivalent of about 83 days performing his Military Reserve duties. While his dual service is admirable, by not charging military or annual leave for some absences, the officer's civilian leave balance exceeded that to which he was entitled. Section 2635.705 of Title 5 of the Code of Federal Regulations states an employee shall use official time in an honest effort to perform official duties. While his civilian leave balance was not reduced while the attorney was performing his official military duties, he received credit as if he was performing his civilian duties at the same time. Further, the agency found the attorney had misused his subordinates' time, using them to schedule personal activities such as haircuts, travel, and golf.

Although the final determination found no dishonesty, lack of integrity, or motive for personal gain on the attorney's part, neither the agency nor the Military Reserve found the attorney's actions acceptable. The attorney was admonished for failure to exercise reasonable care in monitoring his leave balances, and also counseled for misusing subordinates to perform personal tasks. In addition, the Military Reserve Branch counseled him "severely" for his negligence in monitoring his leave account and for improper staff use. Working for two military branches is legal, but it requires careful accounting for your time, including leave.

(Source: Military Service Inspector General)

Director Abused Leave and Personnel, Get's Demoted and Loses Job

The Director of a military staff office caught the eye of the Inspector General by abusing time, attendance, and official travel regulations, and by displaying abusive personal behavior towards her staff.

The Director failed to use proper leave or to document authorized absences involving several trips. She also discouraged attempts by her subordinates to verify her whereabouts, often using profane language and threatening verbal outbursts. In addition, the Inspector General discovered the Director had covered the documents that detailed her use of leave with cross outs, changes and other ink annotations, making them virtually incomprehensible.

As a result, the service secretary took action that resulted in her being removed from the Senior Executive Services and demoted in grade to GS-15. As part of a negotiated settlement, the Director agreed to retire from Federal service as soon as she was eligible.

(Source: Military Service Inspector General)

Travel Violations

Bermuda, Jamaica, Oh I Want to Take You
A certain military general had a fancy for lavish vacations. He decided to take numerous personal trips including one to Bermuda using a military airplane. Once his vacation regimen was discovered, the general was required to reimburse the government for $82,000. In addition, he was demoted upon retirement.

A Private Jet? Don't Mind if I Do …
An O-9 with over 35 years of service in the U.S. military was scheduled for a command visit to a base. His original C-12 flight was delayed, so his staff spontaneously arranged a substitute flight for him: a C-5 that had been previously unscheduled to fly. Despite his many years of experience and his stated commitment to confronting travel abuse issues within his command, he and three members of his staff boarded a near-empty jet to make the command visit on time. The government incurred $38,000 in additional costs for the special flight. The officer was counseled by his command about the violation.

Fasten Your Seatbelts. We're in for a Career-Ending Ride
A Service Colonel was found guilty of larceny and submitting false statements after he used government funds to purchase round trip airline tickets from Kuwait to the States to attend his son's graduation. The Colonel also submitted a false travel authorization listing a fictitious reason for the travel. The Colonel voluntarily repaid the funds and retired early.

False Travel Expenses
A service member filed a travel voucher, falsely claiming expenses for driving from Virginia to California to relocate for a new assignment – and she received pay for 10 days of

per diem. The inquiry found that the service member actually received a ride to Illinois from a friend – and then flew from Illinois to California. She was made to repay the difference in reimbursements and received a letter of reprimand.

German Holiday

Two employees of a DoD Agency obtained overpayment for official travel to Germany. The two employees – whom we will call by the pseudonyms John and Sarah – claimed hotel lodging reimbursement for a night in which they were on a plane flying to Germany.

In addition, the two took a "rest day" before the conference on which no mission duties were performed and no leave was taken. (They indicated that this was in order to overcome jet lag before the conference.) Their misconduct continued after the conference. The two remained in Germany for an extra day to visit various tourist sites in Germany – on the Government's dime – traveling approximately 500 miles in a Government rental car. On their travel vouchers, they requested reimbursement for the fuel costs associated with their personal activity – as well as lodging and per diem expenses.

Sarah later outdid John by claiming hotel costs for the night after she returned to the US and during which she was in her own home.

John and Sarah had over $650 and over $1100 respectively withheld from their pay. The two were also required to receive refresher training on the use of the Defense Travel System. John, the approving official for the travel vouchers for Sarah's trip, was also found to have failed to exercise due diligence as a Certifying Official.

In the background of the case was a romantic relationship between John and Sarah. Though the two denied having a romantic relationship during their trip, they admitted to beginning a relationship eight months later – and that continued. As a result of the ongoing relationship, John was required to recuse himself from all actions involving Sarah, including signing as the approving official for any actions that could be to her benefit or detriment.

Abuse of Official Travel and Leave Garners One Year Probation

The former Deputy Under-Secretary in the Department of Education wound up in Federal court after investigators uncovered discrepancies regarding his travel, leave, and financial disclosure. Investigators discovered that the official, who was also employed as a traveling judge in the State of Texas, had made at least fourteen trips on Government expense when the purpose of his travel was at least partly to accrue time toward a Texas state pension. On several of these trips, the official had additionally requested and received Federal sick leave; further, he collected reimbursement from the Government for some of his personal expenses. Finally, the official failed to report his salary from the State of Texas on his Government financial disclosure form.

The official pled guilty to the conflict of interest statute. He was sentenced to one year of probation, 100 hours of community service, and a $5,000 fine. He also reimbursed the Government $8,659.85 for his fraudulent claims.

Military Officer Dances While the Public Pays

The Facts: According to a military service Inspector General inquiry, a senior military officer planned to attend two balls taking place within roughly an hour's drive of his station. For these, he obtained official orders and, according to his travel claims, received payment for hotel lodging, meals, and incidental expenses (per diem) —amounting all told to around $500. This conduct occurred as one of a series of offenses that resulted in the officer being relieved of command, issued a punitive letter of reprimand, and ordered to forfeit $1,000.

The Law: The Department of Defense (DoD) Travel Regulations provide various guidelines for travel of uniformed (in Volume 1) and civilian (in Volume 2) DoD employees. Applicable to this case was Volume 1: "Joint Federal Travel Regulations" (JFTR). JFTR section U2010 requires a uniformed service member to use the same care in incurring expenses when the Federal Government is to pay "as would a prudent person traveling at personal expense . . . Excess costs, circuitous routes, delays or luxury accommodations that are unnecessary or unjustified are the member's financial responsibility." Moreover, JFTR section U4102 forbids a uniformed service member from obtaining per diem for any temporary duty (TDY) performed within twelve hours. Since attendance at each ball along with round-trip travel could have been completed within twelve hours had the officer exercised prudence, this regulation made it even clearer that the officer should not have obtained his per diem. Since other agencies have travel regulations, all Federal employees are encouraged to verify the propriety of having the Government pay for their travel expenses.

Bumped Well

It was the young employee's first official trip to Washington, DC. It was just a one-day, round trip. Her meeting was scheduled for 1:00 PM. Anxious to make a good impression (and to look around DC), she booked an early-morning flight out of Atlanta. When she got to the airport, she discovered that the flight was overbooked, and the airline was offering free, round-trip tickets to anyone who would volunteer to take the next flight. That flight was to arrive in DC at 12:20 PM, and she figured that she would still have time to make her meeting. As her plane reached Richmond, the pilot announced that would be a slight delay while Air Force One took off. Her plane circled and circled. The delay lasted for over an hour, and by the time the plane finally landed, she had missed the meeting.

FBI Undercover Parties

According to an FBI report, upon the retirement of a senior FBI official, FBI personnel from around the country journeyed to Washington to attend the official's retirement party. Many out-of-town G-men traveled on official orders and public expense. According to their travel orders, the purpose of the trip was to attend an ethics conference! According to the news report, only five people actually attended the ethics forum.

FBI False Travel Claim

A former supervisory special agent of the FBI was sentenced in U.S. District Court for falsely claiming travel expenses to which he was not entitled. The former agent pled guilty to one count of theft of Government property. The former agent had ended a period of travel five days earlier than his schedule (and later travel claim) stated. He was ordered to pay $1,887 in restitution.

Official Travel to Conference Turns into Florida Vacation

A Department of Defense (DoD) official was to travel to and attend a conference in Florida while on DoD travel orders. His wife accompanied him. It was alleged that after checking in at the hotel where the conference was to be held and then renting a convertible, the official promptly left for a short vacation with his wife for all three days of the conference. After an investigation it was determined that the official did not attend the conference, told a subordinate to "cover for him," and filed a fraudulent travel claim with DoD for the three days of the conference he did not attend. A proposal was made to have the official separated from Federal service.

False Travel Claim Filed I

Allegations were made against a Navy enlisted man for filing a false travel claim. After an investigation, it was determined the individual had claimed that his two children accompanied him during his PCS move across the country. In fact, the children were in the custody of his ex-wife. He was reduced in rank one grade and ordered to forfeit $2140 in pay.

False Travel Claim Filed II

It was determined after an investigation that a Department of Defense (DoD) official filed a false claim for travel expenses. The official claimed he was staying at a hotel, and as a result, was paid the appropriate per diem rate by the Navy. It was determined during the course of the investigation that the official had actually been on board a Navy ship (a situation where a much reduced per diem is paid) during the time he claimed he was staying at the hotel. The official reimbursed the Navy, was issued a letter of caution, and was counseled by his supervisor.

False Travel Claim Filed III

A former Department of Defense (DoD) employee was sentenced in U.S. District Court for making false relocation claims to the Government. The former employee made over $15,000 in false relocation claims in connection with a permanent change of station (PCS) move. The judge sentenced the former employee to two years probation and ordered her to pay more than $15,000 in restitution.

False Travel Claim Filed IV

An Army employee was sentenced in U.S. District Court for falsifying lodging expenses. She pled guilty to one count of theft of Government property. The employee had traveled to a nearby facility and incurred no lodging expenses. However, she had filed a claim for $105 when she returned back to her duty station. The employee was sentenced to one year of probation and was ordered to pay a $3,000 fine. Ironically, the employee was the director of the Honesty, Ethics, Accountability, Respect, Trust, and Support (HEARTS) Program for her duty station at the time she committed the violation.

Senior Officer, Who Abused Travel and Misused Staff, Disciplined

A senior military officer and his wife accrued improper airfare expenses by flying in premium class on official business trips. On one trip, for example, the officer justified business-class seats by indicating he was required to perform official business immediately after his arrival at his travel destination, when in fact he spent almost his first full day attending a VIP welcome, making U.S. embassy calls, enjoying lunch and dinner, and touring a local vineyard. The officer explained that he chose to fly business-class on another trip because flying coach would have looked "strange" to his hosts. On other trips, the officer made unofficial, unscheduled stops for family reasons, such as attending his children's sporting events, without taking leave.

Federal travel regulations limit official travel to coach-class unless special circumstances, such as special security requirements, medical requirements, or unavailability of coach-class seats, exist. The rank of the traveler does not justify premium class travel.

The officer also violated 5 C.F.R. 2635.705(b), which mandates a Government employee "shall not encourage, direct, coerce, or request a subordinate to use official time to perform activities other than those required in the performance of official duties or authorized in accordance with law or regulation." Although never issuing any direct orders, the officer requested his subordinates to perform many personal services such as caring for his dog, shopping for athletic gear, and repairing his bicycle. Subordinates reported they had given tours around the local area to the officer's friends and relatives and rescued the officer's wife on the roadside one Sunday. The officer's other violations included asking his subordinates to make thousands of dollars in payments out of their personal funds for various purchases for him. Even though he reimbursed them later, it is improper to solicit loans from subordinates.

The officer received a Punitive Letter of Reprimand at non-judicial punishment proceedings. He voluntarily reimbursed the Government $14,461.03 for travel benefits he and his wife received and charged 15 days to leave to account for days of TAD travel that were for personal business. Further audit of his travel claims resulted in collecting another $1,317. In addition, he was reduced in grade upon retirement from active duty.

(Source: Military Service Inspector General)

False Travel Claim Filed V

A former Department of Defense employee was sentenced in U.S. District Court for submitting false travel claims in relation to a permanent change of station (PCS) move. The former employee was charged with claiming over $22,000 in false travel expenses. She was also charged with altering documents to substantiate the expenses. The judge sentenced her to five years probation and ordered her to pay $10,456 in restitution.

Government Employee Liable for Accident Incurred on Personal Business

A NASA employee on official business arranged to have his return date extended so that he could remain in the area for personal reasons. During his extended stay, he retained his Government-leased rental vehicle. While on his way to the airport to return home, the employee was involved in a car accident when an elk ran into his vehicle. The employee reimbursed the rental car company for more than $2500 in repair costs, and then submitted a reimbursement request to NASA. NASA refused payment as the employee was not on official business at the time of the accident.

The Federal Travel Regulation mandates that an agency may pay only those expenses essential to the transaction of official business. Specifically, employees may be reimbursed for deductibles paid to rental car companies only if the damage occurs while the employee is performing official business. After the NASA employee's temporary duty ended, the rental car became both his expense and his responsibility.

Made in the USA
San Bernardino, CA
24 March 2017